DATE DUE

Aug 14 '68			
Feb 5 '70			
GAYLORD			PRINTED IN U.S.A.

JAPAN 1931–1945

Militarism, Fascism, Japanism?

PROBLEMS IN ASIAN CIVILIZATIONS

UNDER THE EDITORIAL DIRECTION OF THE COMMITTEE ON ORIENTAL
STUDIES, COLUMBIA UNIVERSITY

EDITORIAL COMMITTEE: *Wm. Theodore de Bary,* COLUMBIA UNIVERSITY • *Ainslie T. Embree,* COLUMBIA UNIVERSITY • *John Meskill,* BARNARD COLLEGE • *Johanna M. Menzel,* VASSAR COLLEGE • *Arthur Tiedemann,* THE CITY COLLEGE OF NEW YORK

WANG AN-SHIH—Practical Reformer? *Edited by John Meskill*

THE CHINESE CIVIL SERVICE—CAREER OPEN TO TALENT? *Edited by Johanna M. Menzel*

DEMOCRACY IN MODERN JAPAN—GROUNDWORK OR FAÇADE? *Edited by George O. Totten*

JAPAN 1931–1945—MILITARISM, FASCISM, JAPANISM? *Edited by Ivan Morris*

1857 IN INDIA—MUTINY OR WAR OF INDEPENDENCE? *Edited by Ainslie T. Embree*

Other volumes in preparation

JAPAN 1931–1945

Militarism, Fascism, Japanism?

EDITED WITH AN INTRODUCTION BY

Ivan Morris

COLUMBIA UNIVERSITY

D . C . HEATH AND COMPANY · BOSTON

Library of Congress Catalog Card number 63-12802

COPYRIGHT © 1963 BY D. C. HEATH AND COMPANY

*No part of the material covered by this copyright may be reproduced
in any form without written permission of the publisher.* (6 I 3)

PRINTED IN THE UNITED STATES OF AMERICA

Table of Contents

v

458C— 30

Introduction

ONE of the difficulties in discussing the 1931–1945 period in Japan is that of nomenclature. Few people would disagree about referring to Italy between 1922 and 1944 as "Fascist" or to Germany between 1933 and 1945 as "Nazi." But when it comes to Japan there is no generally accepted word to denote the corresponding era. It has been termed, *inter alia,* ultra-nationalist, fascist, totalitarian, militarist and Japanist. Each of these descriptions has its drawbacks.

"Ultra-nationalism," though widely used in relation to pre-war Japan, does not lend itself to simple definition, and there is still no consensus about its real meaning. A distinguished political scientist from Japan has discussed the question of why in his country nationalism evokes epithets like "ultra" and "extreme":

The distinction that may first come to mind is the presence of expansionist, militarist tendencies. The trouble is that during the period when nation-states first came into existence *all* the countries that were under absolutist regimes blatantly carried out wars of external aggression; in other words, a tendency to military expansion was an inherent impulse in nationalism long before the so-called age of imperialism in the nineteenth century. It is quite true that in Japan nationalism was guided by this impulse to a stronger degree and that it manifested it in a clearer way than in other countries. But this is merely a matter of quantity. Quite apart from any difference in degree, there is a qualitative difference in the inner motive power that spurred Japan to expansion abroad and to oppression at home; and it is only owing to this qualitative difference that Japanese nationalism acquired the "ultra" aspect.[1]

Now, when we come to analyze this qualitative difference, we find that it involves concepts fundamental to political thought and psychology in Japan since the Meiji Restoration. Though ultra-nationalism appeared in some of its most blatant manifestations during the years with which we are concerned, it has been an underlying approach for almost the entire modern period.

"Fascism" has lost much of its semantic value since it came to be bandied about as a pejorative to describe unpopular people or ideas. The term is still meaningful when carefully used in concrete contexts like "the West European form of fascist government in the 1930's," but whether it can correctly be applied to Japan without some very careful qualifications is a moot point. Since one of the common approaches to understanding what happened in pre-war Japan is a comparison with Nazi Germany, and to a lesser extent with Fascist Italy, and since the word "fascism" is a great favourite with certain writers, we shall find it cropping up frequently in the selections that follow. A major question for the reader to decide will be whether Japan of the 1931–45 period does in fact fit into the general pattern of European fascism and, if not, where the essential difference lies. It should be noted that the language contains no word for "fascism" and that Japanese

[1] Maruyama Masao, *Thought and Behaviour in Modern Japanese Politics,* Ivan Morris, ed., Oxford, 1963, pp. 2–3.

writers are obliged to resort to the ungainly phonetic equivalent, *fu-a-shi-zu-mu.*

The period is sometimes described as "totalitarian." This is misleading. Much as the military leaders, and especially the Tōjō government, may have wished to reorganize Japan on totalitarian lines, they were always bedevilled by the pluralism of power in Japan and, despite repeated efforts and much exhortation, never achieved the degree of political coordination and mobilization of energies that we find, for instance, in Nazi Germany. The more we examine the realities of pre-war and wartime Japan, the more we are struck by the failure to attain that unity about which so many pious words were spoken and so many stirring slogans coined.[2]

"Militarist" is an ambiguous term which can refer either to a country's objectives (i.e. a policy of military strength and expansion) or to the nature of its leadership (i.e. government by military men) or to both. Japan pursued a militarist policy for a considerable part of her modern period; and, as political practice evolved under the Meiji Constitution, the military enjoyed certain advantages (notably the power to force the resignation of the Cabinet and to veto the formation of any new Cabinet not to their liking) that gave them a stranglehold over civilian governments. In the early 1930's the strength of the military came to supersede that of the civilian leadership, but it was not until about 1940 that civil authority entirely collapsed and Japan became, properly speaking, a *militarist* state. To describe the entire period by this term represents an oversimplification of a complex, many-staged process.

Still other observers stress the uniqueness of the Japanese experience and prefer to define the period by terms like "Japanism" (*Nihon-shugi*) or "Emperor System" (*Tennō Sei*) that emphasize the

fundamental divergence from Western patterns. Japan's wartime leaders and propagandists were at pains to stress the qualitative difference between their government and those of their European allies. Addressing the Diet in 1943 the Prime Minister, General Tōjō, declared,

> People often refer to this as a dictatorial government, but I should like to make the matter clear. . . . The man called Tōjō is no more than a single humble subject. I am just the same as you. The only difference is that I have been given the responsibility of being Prime Minister. . . . It is only when I am exposed to the light of His Majesty that I shine. Were it not for this light, I should be no better than a pebble by the roadside. It is because I enjoy the confidence of His Majesty and occupy my present position that I shine. This puts me in a completely different category from those European rulers who are known as dictators.[3]

A reading of the selections in his book may possibly lead to the conclusion that some term like "ultra-Japanism" comes closest to characterizing the period in question.

Rather than prejudge the issue by giving my own designation of the period, I have simply described it by the dates, 1931 to 1945. Even this may require some justification. There can be little doubt about the terminal date, 1945, when Japan suffered the first great defeat in her history and when the entire ideological structure that had been built up over so long a period of time and with so much sound and fury collapsed like an elaborate house of bamboo.

When it comes to the beginning of the period, however, we find no such clearcut line of demarcation as is provided by the March on Rome, for example, or by Hitler's appointment as Chancellor. 1931, the year of the Manchurian invasion, can be taken to mark the beginning of the decline of civilian government and of the rapid rise

---

[2] E.g. General Araki's "a hundred million hearts beating like one."

[3] Quoted by Maruyama, *op. cit.* p. 17.

to power of the military. Yet the events that exploded with such dramatic force after 1931 — terror and assassination at home, aggressive moves on the Continent, new international alignments — had all been adumbrated in the previous "preparatory" period.[4] No single year can be taken to mark a revolution in Japanese foreign policy or in her domestic power relations. The gradation of Japan's move toward ultra-rightist control is a characteristic that distinguishes it from the corresponding European experiences.

[4] Professor Maruyama refers to 3 periods: (1) 1919–31 preparatory period: right-wing movements among civilians, suppressive legislation against the left; (2) 1931–36 mature period: the military become the driving force in the right-wing movements; attempted *coups d'état*, "incidents," etc.; (3) 1936–45 consummation period: the military openly assume power and lead Japan into a clash with the West.

The selections in this book have been grouped under three "model" points of view according to which the turbulent period is characterized as: I, militarist; II, fascist; and III Japanist. This is a matter of emphasis and of convenience. It is rare to find a writer who subscribes totally and exclusively to any one of the approaches that is pointed out in the statement at the head of each section. Since the division is artificial, the selections are unlikely to fit neatly into any single category; often they contain arguments that apply to two, or even to all three, of the approaches. The quotations themselves have been chosen not so much to represent the "model" points of view as to provide a basis for discussing these views. It is hoped that the division into sections, arbitrary though it is, will help to organize this discussion and make it more fruitful.

Writings about Japan are bound to include several proper names and terms that are unfamiliar to most Western readers. These are briefly explained in a Glossary at the front of the book. A simple chronology has also been provided to date the principal events mentioned in the selections.

I am grateful to Oxford University Press for allowing me to use translations included in Professor Maruyama's Thought and Behaviour in Modern Japanese Politics *and to Columbia University Press for permitting extensive quotations from* Sources of the Japanese Tradition. *I should also like to acknowledge Professor George O. Totten's help in planning this book.*

GLOSSARY

AMATERASU ŌMIKAMI   The Shinto Sun Goddess and ancestral divinity of the Japanese Imperial family.

ARAKI SADAO* (b. 1877)   An extreme militarist who played a prominent role in the 1930s as a general and member of the Imperial Way Faction of the Army. He served as War Minister and was an active supporter of the Manchurian Incident of 1931. Later he was Education Minister and had considerable influence on nationalist education. Araki was tried as a Class A war criminal and sentenced to life imprisonment; he was released in 1955 owing to ill health.

BLACK DRAGON SOCIETY (KOKURYŪ KAI)   More correctly known as the Amur River Association, this was an aggressive nationalist group which was founded in 1901 and continued until the end of the war. Its programme emphasized Japan's leadership in Asia as a harmonizer of Eastern and Western culture, foreign expansion, especially in Northern Manchuria, cultivation of the virtues of the Yamato race based on national polity education, and internal reform.

BLOOD PLEDGE CORPS INCIDENT (KETSUMEI DAN JIKEN)   An attempt in February 1932 by a fanatic agrarian radical society to remove the ruling clique, whom they considered to be responsible for agrarian suffering and national weakness. The plans called for the assassination of certain political and business leaders; about 20 prospective victims were listed and each one assigned to a specific member of the Corps for disposal. Only 2 of the planned assassinations were actually carried out — those of the Finance Minister and the director of the Mitsui Company.

EDUCATION RESCRIPT   The Imperial Rescript on Education, which was issued in 1890, had the force of holy writ until Japan's defeat in 1945. Enunciating traditional moral principles and stressing the Confucian virtues, such as filial piety and obedience, it also stressed the need for loyalty and self-sacrifice in the service of the Emperor. The Rescript was regularly read aloud with great ceremony in schools and colleges.

EIGHT CORNERS OF THE WORLD UNDER ONE ROOF (HAKKŌ ICHIU)   An ancient phrase taken up by the extreme nationalists to suggest that the unity of the world must be achieved under Japan's leadership. In its more moderate sense it represented a vague ideal of world brotherhood.

EMPEROR SYSTEM   An ideal of government, represented by the extreme nationalists as being uniquely Japanese, according to which the entire nation is loyally united under a divine and all-powerful Emperor.

FEBRUARY INCIDENT   Carried out on February 26, 1936, in Tokyo, this was the most nearly successful of all the pre-war attempted *coups d'état*. It took the form of a major uprising by the militant Imperial Way Faction of the Army, with the aim of overcoming the Control Faction, destroying the ruling elite and thus effecting a thorough reform of the national structure. After assassinating several important government leaders, the insurgents barricaded themselves in one part of the city; martial law was proclaimed, and after 3 days the rebels surrendered at the personal command of the Emperor. Subsequently 13 Army officers and 4 civilians (including the national-socialist leader, Kita Ikki) were executed, and several leading military figures

* Names are given in the normal Japanese order, i.e., with the family name first.

xi

were removed from positions of authority. The incident failed to accomplish its specific objectives, but greatly encouraged the trend towards totalitarianism and Army control.

GONDŌ SEIKYŌ or NARIAKI (1868–1937) A widely travelled historian and right-wing activist, Mr. Gondō participated in the Chinese revolution of 1911 when he was in Shanghai. After returning to Tokyo he wrote "The Principles of Autonomy under the Emperor." The foremost spokesman of a purely agrarian nationalism in the 1920s, Gondō demanded a return to agrarian autonomy and an agrarian-centred economy. His thinking was influential among the younger officers.

GOTŌ AKINORI One of the activists in the May 15 Incident of 1932 in which the Prime Minister, Mr. Inukai, was assassinated.

GREAT JAPAN PRODUCTION PARTY (DAI NIHON SEISAN TŌ) In June 1931 this party was formed in an effort to unify all elements of the extreme right-wing movement. It claimed a membership of 100,000 soon after its founding. The party's programme emphasized a strong foreign policy under the banner of "Greater Japan." It was also responsible for bringing or establishing labour unions and organizations within the rightist fold.

HASHIMOTO KINGORŌ (1890–1957) Army officer and leader of an extremist young officers' association in the 1930s. A militant xenophobe, Hashimoto was responsible for the shelling of H.M.S. Ladybird and U.S.S. Panay on the Yangtse in 1937. He organized various ultra-nationalist societies in the late 1930s. In 1948 he was sentenced to life imprisonment as a Class A war criminal, but he was released in 1955.

HEAVEN-SENT SOLDIERS' UNIT INCIDENT (SHIMPEI TAI JIKEN) An ambitious military-civilian attempt in 1933 to carry out the objectives of the May 15 Incident of 1932 by assassinating a number of leading figures. The police heard about the plot and arrested the conspirators in time.

INOUE NISSHŌ (b.1886) A priest of extreme rightist beliefs, who before turning to Buddhism had spent most of his life on the continent as a secret agent for the Japanese army. On his return to Japan he organized several extreme nationalist societies. The most important of these was the Blood Pledge Corps, which was responsible for the killing in 1932 of the Finance Minister and of the director of Mitsui. As a result he was sentenced to life imprisonment; but he was released in 1940 on a general amnesty.

INUKAI TSUYOSHI or KI (1885–1932) Prominent political leader who became Prime Minister in 1931 and who was assassinated in the following year in the May 15 Incident.

JAPANISM (NIHONSHUGI) A vague term, used mainly by people of strong nationalist persuasion to emphasize the uniqueness and superiority of Japan's social, political and cultural heritage. In the 1930s Japanism, with its stress on self-sacrifice and loyalty to the family and State, was frequently contrasted with the "egoism" and individualism of democracy.

KAWAKAMI JŌTARŌ (b.1889) A Christian and a founder of the Japan Labour-Farmer Party in 1926, Kawakami was subsequently active in the socialist movement up to the present.

KITA IKKI (1884–1937) Leading right-wing revolutionary and writer. He was a powerful advocate of national socialism and is frequently described as the founder of modern Japanese fascism. He demanded a radical change in Japanese society and the promotion of revolution in Asia under the aegis of Japan. Kita was executed after the failure of the February Incident of 1936, on which he was believed to have had great influence. The "General Outline of Measures for the Reconstruction of Japan" (*Nihon Kaizō Hōan*), which Kita wrote in 1919, was printed and circulated secretly. Though banned by the police, it exerted a great effect on the nationalist movement. Its domestic programme included the nationalization of major industries, an eight-hour workday and a limit on incomes.

KOGA KIYOSHI Ringleader of the assassins in the May 15 Incident of 1932, he fatally wounded the Prime Minister, Mr. Inukai.

KONUMA TADASHI (b.1912) A member of the Blood Pledge Corps, Konuma assassinated the former Finance Minister in 1932. He was sentenced to life imprisonment, but released a few years later.

MAKINO NOBUAKI (1861–1949) Active in both diplomatic and domestic affairs, Count Makino was a close adviser to the Throne and one of the most influential leaders of his time.

MARUYAMA MASAO (b.1914) Professor of Tokyo University, who has specialized in the study of Japanese political thought. He is best known for his work on the influence of neo-Confucianism and on the development of nationalist thought in the modern period. During the post-war period he has been one of the principal intellectual mentors of the "progressive" movement in Japan.

MATSUI IWANE (1878–1948) Supreme commander in the Shanghai region in 1937. The outrages in Nanking took place during his term of responsibility, and he was hanged as a war criminal.

MAY 15 INCIDENT An attempted *coup d'état* with the same general purpose as the Blood Pledge Corps Incident and carried out in 1932 by the same type of agrarian fanatics with the help of certain young officers. The plans were to assassinate political and business leaders, as well as certain statesmen close to the Throne; it was hoped that the army would then take over. The Prime Minister, Mr. Inukai, was killed, but the *coup* collapsed owing mainly to lack of support from the army.

MEIJI CONSTITUTION Constitution promulgated in 1889 as a "gift" to the Japanese people from the Emperor. It stated that the Emperor was the head of the State and that all rights of sovereignty were invested in him. The most important innovation of the Meiji Constitution was to establish a bicameral parliament (Diet).

MEIJI EMPEROR (1852–1912) Mutsuhito, the 122nd Sovereign of Japan (r.1868–1912), who came to the Throne at the crucial time when power was transferred from the Tokugawa shogunate to the Emperor (or rather, to those who acted in the Emperor's name). His reign covered the decades during which Japan was transformed from a feudal state into a modern, centralized power capable of competing with Western nations on their own terms.

MEIJI RESTORATION The transfer of power in 1868 from the Tokugawa shogunate to the Emperor and his advisers; also refers to the period of transformation that followed (see Meiji Emperor).

MINAMI JIRŌ (1874–1955) Prominent military figure, who served as War Minister, C.-in-C. of the Kwantung Army and Governor-General of Korea. He was sentenced to life imprisonment in the war crimes trials.

MINSEI TŌ and SEIYŪ KAI The two major political parties in the decade or so prior to the Second World War. The parties were never able to establish firmly the principle of party government, and they fought a losing battle with growing military authoritarianism in the 1930s, until they were finally dissolved in 1940.

MIYAKE SETSUREI (1860–1945) A prominent journalist who during the late Meiji period was a severe critic of Japan's excessive Westernization and a strong advocate of nationalism.

MURANAKA KŌJI (1903–1936) One of the young officers who participated in the ultra-nationalist incidents of the early 1930s. He was executed for his role in the February Incident of 1936.

ŌKAWA SHŪMEI (1886–1957) A jurist, specialist in Oriental philosophy and one of the most prominent civilians in the pre-war rightist movement. He maintained close connexions with high military and bureaucratic circles as well as with professional nationalists, and he founded many rightist societies. In the 1930s he was a prominent participant in several of the incidents.

RŌNIN Originally referred to disenfeoffed samurai, but later came to apply in general to adventurers, soldiers of fortune and others who lived by their wits, courage, and readiness to break the law.

SERVE-THE-STATE-THROUGH-INDUSTRY MOVEMENT or INDUSTRIAL PATRIOTIC MOVEMENT (SAMPŌ UNDŌ) Labour movement founded in 1937, on the model of the Nazi *Arbeitsfront,* to unite the efforts of Japanese labour behind the war effort. Branches were established in factories and plants throughout the country.

SHIGA JŪKŌ A conservative who deplored the extreme Westernization of Japan during the early Meiji period.

SHŌWA PERIOD Reign of Emperor Hirohito, who came to the Throne in 1926.

SHŌWA RESTORATION A term invented by the revolutionary right wing in the late 1920s signifying a plan of action to "restore" the country to its ancient virtues under the authority of the Emperor.

SOCIALIST MASSES' PARTY (SHAKAI TAISHŪ TŌ) Amalgamation of several moderate proletarian parties, formed in 1932 with a programme of opposing capitalism, communism, and fascism. It lost some leaders as it gradually moved towards the right, until it voluntarily disbanded in 1940.

SOCIETY TO CARRY OUT HEAVEN'S WAY ON EARTH (GYŌJI SHA) Influential rightist society established in 1924 by Ōkawa Shūmei. The society attempted to combine the agrarian and the nationalist-socialist strains in the rightist movement, and it built up a working relationship between civilian nationalists and young officers in the army.

TACHIBANA KŌSABURŌ (b.1893) A native of the economically depressed area to the northeast of Tokyo, Tachibana was an important figure in the agrarian movement of the early 1930s. He was involved in the plot surrounding the assassination of Mr. Inukai in 1932.

TAISHŌ PERIOD Reign of Emperor Yoshihito, from 1912 to 1926.

TŌGŌ SHIGENORI (1882–1950) Prominent diplomat who was serving as Foreign Minister at the outbreak of the Pacific War. He resigned in 1942, but later returned to the government and was active in persuading his colleagues to accept the Allied terms of surrender.

TŌJŌ HIDEKI (1884–1948) Prime Minister of Japan and virtual dictator during the Second World War. He resigned in 1944 after the fall of Saipan. Tōjō was hanged in 1948 as a major war criminal.

TOKUGAWA Name of the family of Shōguns who from 1603 to 1868 ruled Japan hereditarily, being in theory the agents of the reigning Emperors.

TOKUTOMI SOHŌ (1863–1957) Critic, journalist, and author. At one time both a Christian and a democrat, he turned against Western democracy and co-operated with the militarists in favour of Emperor-centred nationalism.

YAMATO Name of a district in western Japan where the first Emperors held Court. Later it came to be applied to the entire country, and it is often used as a patriotic or poetic synonym for Nihon (Japan).

YOSHIDA SHIGERU (b.1878) Diplomat and politician, who was appointed to be Ambassador to London in 1936 but who later fell into disfavour with the militarists owing to his reputation as a liberal. After the war Mr. Yoshida formed 5 conservative cabinets and remained Prime Minister during most of the 1946–53 period.

CHRONOLOGY

1868	Meiji Restoration.
1889	Promulgation of Meiji Constitution.
1904–5	Russo-Japanese War.
1931 (Sept.)	Manchurian Incident.
1932 (Feb.-Mar.)	Blood Pledge Corps Incident.
1932 (May)	May 15 Incident.
1933 (July)	Heaven-Sent Soldiers' Unit Incident.
1936 (Feb.)	February 26 Incident.
1941 (Dec.)	Attack on Pearl Harbour.
1945 (Aug.)	Surrender of Japan.

MILITARISM

"Throughout the 1930's the bureaucrats kept up the appearance of being in the political saddle, balancing the party politicians and big business interests against the militarists; but as the politicians and big business interests lost power, it was more and more evident that the militarists, if not in the saddle, were at least leading the horse."

— Edwin O. Reischauer

"These uniformed politicians [Japan's militarists] coupled their pleas for the adoption of anti-British and anti-American policies with enticing proposals to eliminate existing social and political evils at home, and to establish a new order of things in the Japanese homeland. In fact, the course of action to which they finally committed the nation drove Japan into the Axis camp and precipitated the greatest disaster ever suffered by the nation. For this — and the defeat and universal misery which their policies visited upon my nation — they must be held responsible."

— Yoshida Shigeru

"Of this program [of the militarists] we may say, with the poet, that it is as 'simple as the cow's lowing.' "

— Tanin and Yohan

FASCISM

". . . a sweeping reform of the imperial court in the spirit of the Emperor Jimmu in founding the state and in the spirit of the great Meiji emperor will be carried out. The present Privy Councillors and other officials will be dismissed from their posts, and in their place will come talent, sought throughout the realm, capable of assisting the Emperor."

— Kita Ikki

"The fascist parties in western Europe are, in their composition, petty-bourgeois parties. Their leading strata . . . are to a large extent landowners, but they pursue a policy of defending the interests of finance capital, which represents the leading force of a capitalist society which has reached the stage of monopoly capitalism. And the same holds true of Japan, although the leading rôle in the fascist movement of that country is played by the landowners and the higher bureaucracy."

— Karl Radek

"The Japanese fascist movement naturally had elements in common with the fascist ideology current in the world. It shared the ideology of its Italian and German counterparts in such matters as the rejection of the world view of individualistic liberalism, opposition to parliamentary politics which is the political expression of liberalism, insistence on foreign expansion, a tendency to glorify military build-up and war, a strong emphasis on racial myths and the national essence . . ."

— MARUYAMA MASAO

JAPANISM

"Our contributions to the world lie only in giving full play more than ever to our Way which is of the Japanese people. The people must more than ever create and develop a new Japan by virtue of their immutable national polity which is the basis of the State and by virtue of the Way of the Empire which stands firm throughout the ages at Home and abroad, and thereby more than ever guard and maintain the prosperity of the Imperial Throne which is coeval with heaven and earth. This, indeed, is our mission."

— KOKUTAI NO HONGI

"In its actual functional value to modern Japan, the primitive [Shinto] solar mythology has been modified and enlarged by the influence of social and political patterns and impressed by the ulterior motives of tribal, dynastic, and racial aggrandizement, until, reshaped into its modern politico-religious mold, it becomes the symbol of the eternal state."

— D. C. HOLTOM

"The fundamental essence of the Japanese system of government is the unity of high and low, of the Monarch and his people. This points clearly to the aim of the Japanese, which amounts to the glorification of the Emperor, for which purpose public welfare must take precedence over private, personal welfare . . . The present difficult situation cannot be overcome until the Japanese people will be inspired with the desire to realize with maximum determination its great ideal of world significance. Without this inspiration it is impossible either to solve the Manchuro-Mongolian problem or that of continental policy. . . . It is a superficial view or a curious distortion of reality to imagine that Japan is a militaristic country . . ."

— ARAKI SADAO

"The Japanese empire is a manifestation of morality and its special characteristic is the propagation of the Imperial Way . . . It is necessary to foster the increased power of the empire, to cause East Asia to return to its original form of independence and co-prosperity by shaking off the yoke of Europe and America, and to let its countries and peoples develop their respective abilities in peaceful cooperation and secure livelihood."

— DRAFT OF BASIC PLAN FOR ESTABLISHMENT OF GREATER EAST ASIA CO-PROSPERITY SPHERE

I. MILITARISM

THE VICTORY OF EXTREMISM IN THE 1930'S WAS THE RESULT OF A CONSPIRACY BY THE MILITARY CLIQUE (*GUMBATSU*) WHO BY TREACHERY AND VIOLENCE SUCCEEDED IN OVERTHROWING THE LIBERAL-DEMOCRATIC FORM OF GOVERNMENT THAT HAD DEVELOPED IN JAPAN SINCE THE END OF THE 19TH CENTURY.*

Summary Statements

The Militarists Provoked the Attack

The above explanation, which is widely supported both in Japan and in the West, reassures the Japanese and their friends abroad that the unpleasantness of 1931–45 was merely a temporary deviation from the main course of Japan's modern development and that it was the responsibility of a wicked minority who "deceived and misled the people of Japan" (Potsdam Declaration, para. 6). If nothing else, the theory has the merit of simplicity. We find it in nutshell form in the editor's preface to the diplomatic record of Mr. Joseph Grew, the United States Ambassador to Japan from 1932 to 1941.

THE decade of the nineteen-twenties found the civilian elements in control of Japanese policy . . . Japanese militarists, however, seeing their control being weakened and their hopes of conquest disappearing, provoked the attack on Manchuria in 1931 to reassert their power both in domestic and foreign affairs.

* For various assessments of pre-war Japanese democracy see *Democracy in Modern Japan: Groundwork or Façade?* in this series.

From the editor's preface to *Turbulent Era* by Joseph Grew (Boston: Houghton Mifflin Co.) Vol II, p. 922.

1

The Manchurian Incident

Mr. John Maki also gives 1931 as the date when the militarists embarked on their campaign to destroy the *status quo* in Japan and to assume power for themselves.

I F a definite date can be placed on the beginning of the major drive of the militarists toward empire and complete domination of Japan, it is probably September 18, 1931, when the "Manchurian Incident" started. The "Manchurian Incident" was not only an expression of the militarists' policy of aggression on the continent, but it also marked the beginning of their campaign to bring Japan itself completely under their control. The invasion of Manchuria really broke the power of the civilian elements as a force in Japanese government.

The seizure of Manchuria from China has been denounced as Japan's first major act of aggression against China, an act which paved the way for the [Pacific] war. However, the internal consequences of the "Incident" were as great as the external ones. If it was an act of aggression against China, then it was also a major step in the direction of the establishment of an authoritarian régime at home.

From *Japanese Militarism* by John M. Maki (New York: Alfred A. Knopf, Inc.), pp. 211–12.

The Militarists Take the Lead

Among the outstanding Western experts on Japan, Professor E. O. Reischauer puts the blame heavily on the militarists.

THE turning point between the liberal 1920's and the reactionary 1930's came in 1931, when certain military forces, without the approval of the civil government and possibly even without the specific approval of higher military authorities, started their own war of territorial aggrandizement. . . . Meanwhile, other military extremists at home had brought a sudden end to party rule by another form of direct action — political assassination. A group of young army and navy officers, claiming they were attempting to free the emperor from evil advisers, assassinated the Premier on May 15, 1932. The government leaders, while condemning this act, tacitly accepted it as judgment against party government, and set up a compromise "National Government" with a cabinet made up of a central bloc of professional bureaucrats, with other contingents from the political parties and the armed forces balancing each other.

This compromise government became typical of the rest of the 1930's. The military element in succeeding cabinets tended to grow and party representatives slowly dwindled in number, but the professional bureaucrats retained the central and, theoretically, the dominant position throughout the decade. However, the militarists definitely took the lead in creating new policies of government. With the success of their Manchurian adventure assured and supported by sporadic acts of terrorism committed by individual extremists, they forced as much of their program as they could on the compromise governments.

By simply refusing to recognize the authority of the Diet over the Cabinet, the militarists robbed the Diet of one power after another, and by the end of the decade they had reduced it to little more than an impotent and very timorous debating society. . . . The militarists also increased the already strong imperialistic and militaristic indoctrination of the people, and they did their best to whip the masses up to a frenzy of nationalistic fervor. . . .

The militarists also sanctioned and encouraged a veritable witchhunt for all persons whose slightest word or deed could be construed to be *lèse majesté*. Liberal educators were forced to resign their academic positions on the grounds that they had handled the imperial rescript on education improperly, and leading statesmen were driven out of political life because of some unfortunate allusion involving an emperor. . . .

Party politicians, of course, fought bitterly to preserve their hold on the government, but the only method they knew was through the ballot-box, and with the de-

From *Japan: Past and Present* by Edwin O. Reischauer, pp. 165–71. Copyright 1947 by Alfred A. Knopf, Inc., and used with their permission.

3

cline of the Diet, elections meant less and less. Whether they won elections or not, the party politicians were gradually losing all control of the government. Some cabinets even excluded party men altogether, and those politicians who did not swing around to timid support of the extreme militarists found it best to abandon political life, or at least to keep silent. . . .

Throughout the 1930's the bureaucrats kept up the appearance of being in the political saddle, balancing the party politicians and big business interests against the militarists; but as the politicians and big business interests lost power, it was more and more evident that the militarists, if not in the saddle, were at least leading the horse.

The Anti-Foreign Militarists

In their accounts of the events of the 1930's Japanese conservative leaders, like the former Prime Minister Mr. Yoshida Shigeru, also tend to blame the militarists, though usually without analyzing the underlying factors that allowed them to achieve such success. Because of his pro-Western reputation Mr. Yoshida was viewed askance by the militarists and for a time he was placed under arrest — a fortunate circumstance, as it turned out, for his later political career. Though in the pre-war context Mr. Yoshida was resented by the nationalists as a liberal, he emerges in the post-war climate, with essentially unchanged views, as a staunch exponent of Japanese conservatism.

CERTAIN groups of people in Japan began to manifest antipathy to Japan's traditional diplomatic policy as early as the days of the Taisho era. The reasons responsible for the display of such sentiments were varied, ranging from simple envy of the wealth and power of Great Britain and the United States to opposition aroused by some of the actions taken by those countries in international affairs. But the most culpable among such critics of Japan's traditional foreign policies, in my opinion, were those who encouraged and exploited anti-foreign feeling in others in order to strengthen their own political position.

The most cogent example of this tendency was the attitude adopted by Japan's militarists at the time of the Manchurian "incident." As I have noted, the anti-American and anti-British feeling among segments within the Japanese Army sprang from differing causes, but it is clear that the primary objective of the various military cliques was the same — to gain power at the expense of those around the Throne and those in responsible positions within the civilian government who advocated a policy of friendship with Great Britain and the United States. These uniformed politicians coupled their pleas for the adoption of anti-British and anti-American policies with enticing proposals to eliminate existing social and political evils at home, and to establish a new order of things in the Japanese homeland. In fact, the course of action to which they finally committed the nation drove Japan into the Axis camp and precipitated the greatest disaster ever suffered by the nation. For this — and the defeat and universal misery which their policies visited upon my nation — they must be held responsible.

From Yoshida Shigeru, *The Yoshida Memoirs,* pp. 9–10 (London: William Heinemann Ltd.).

The Supreme Command

Mr. Shigemitsu Mamoru, Japan's Foreign Minister at the time of the attack on Pearl Harbour and a prominent figure in post-war conservative politics, also puts the blame heavily on the military.

THE supreme power laid down in the [Meiji] Constitution was not personally exercised by the Emperor but laid on the shelf, and power gradually slipped away elsewhere. . . . The development of democracy in Japan lagged and the power of the political parties was small. So between a constitutional monarch of the British type and the nation there was room for an interloper to drive in a wedge.

This state of affairs was welcomed most by the Supreme Command, which functioned independently of the Government and the Diet. During the "Showa upheaval," on many important occasions, they enforced their views in opposition to the will of the Emperor, who was in theory the Supreme Commander. The Emperor did no more than endorse the views of the Supreme Command, learnt before or after the event. Such deification of the Emperor had produced in earlier ages government by the great military houses; in more recent times it produced government by the Supreme Command. Thereby the military were released from the highest and final restraint, intended to keep them under control. In order to grasp the actual power, they preached the independence of the Supreme Command and the doctrine of nationalism, the theory that the Emperor was an organ of state was rejected and the entourage of the Emperor was even persecuted. They planned *coups d'état* and finally resorted to assassination. It might not be right to say that they were consciously implicated in these occurrences but, inasmuch as they aimed directly and indirectly at the realization of military dictatorship, the fact is that the continuation of such measures brought about the accomplishment of their aims.

From Shigemitsu Mamoru, *Japan and Her Destiny*, pp. 51–52 (London: Hutchinson and Company Ltd.).

The Political Program of the Militarists

O. TANIN and E. YOHAN

O. Tanin and E. Yohan, two Russian Marxists writing in the early 1930's, give particular stress to the role of the militarists in determining the course of Japanese politics and suggest that they had a clearly-defined program for Japan's domestic development as well as for her overseas expansion. In what ways does the political viewpoint of these writers influence their approach to the question? Is their view of the Army and its program similar to those of the earlier writers in this section?

T HE program of the militarists re- produces in the simplest and most primitive form precisely those highly aggressive and reactionary features of Japanese imperialism which result from its military-feudal character. This program, according to the statements of the military leaders themselves, may be summed up in three principal propositions.

1. The army is the vanguard of the nation, accordingly, to the army and not to the parliamentary political parties belongs the leadership of the nation's political life. Only the army is able to uphold the dynasty, render the interests of individual groups of the ruling classes subordinate to the interests of the régime as a whole, and promote the spread of the "imperial idea" (*i.e.,* of Japanese aggression) to other countries.

2. The main aim of state policy at the present time should be to carry out the plan of a "Greater Japan," that is, to create a powerful colonial Asiatic empire, in the first place, through the seizure of the territory of Eastern Asia. The foremost enemy, whose opposition must be crushed before this can be achieved, is the Soviet Union.

3. To the aims of foreign aggression must be subordinated the entire home policy, whose principal content must therefore be:

(a) increased government control of industry and finance;

(b) the ending of the acute agricultural crisis, which threatens to assume the proportions of an agrarian revolution, which would sweep away one of the main buttresses of the whole régime: feudal land ownership and with it the monarchy.

(c) merciless, relentless eradication of the "Red danger," that is, of all manifestations of the revolutionary movement in the country.

Of this program we may say, with the poet, that it is as "simple as a cow's lowing." We shall illustrate by quoting the military leaders themselves.

The premise upon which this program rests is, first of all, struggle for the complete concentration of power in the hands of the army.

The reason put forward in advocating the leading rôle of the army in politics, and strongly appealed to, is that the army is the upholder and guardian of the ancient

From O. Tanin and E. Yohan, *Militarism and Fascism in Japan* (New York: International Publishers, 1934), pp. 184–203.

7

traditions, of the code of feudal knight morality (the *busido,* code of moral rules of the Japanese Samurai), of the divine right of the emperor, which cannot be subject to the dictates of political parties, and which can gain a new lease on life only through the army which depends on it alone. One of the military leaders explains that:

The center of the Japanese system of government is indisputably *Tenno* — the emperor. The emperor's will is the will of the state. In Japan there is no opposition between emperor and subjects. The monarchy in Japan is unlimited and all-embracing. The emperor is the center of the state and its complete essence. The monarch represents the height of virtue and virtue is the philosophy of Japan.

Araki explains the regalia which denote the emperor's power:

It is justice (the mirror), mercy (the jasper) and bravery (the sword), represented by the regalias of the Japanese dynasty, that are the fundamental ideals of the Japanese state, the way marked out by the Emperors. This is the so-called "Imperial Course." Japanese history represents nothing but the realization of this course.

Surrounding the monarchy with this aureole the militarists strive to direct the dissatisfaction among the youth of the petty bourgeoisie and other sections of the population with the policy of the government and with the rapaciousness of the barons of high finance into the channel of defense of the monarchy, which after the "second restoration" will, they declare, bring happiness to the Japanese nation and cleanse the social life of the country of mercenary politicians and greedy speculators. Who can uphold this "Imperial Course" but the army? It is clear that only the army is able to defend the national interests and should therefore come forward with a political program of its own. Lieutenant-General Tamon recently wrote

Our influence in Manchuria would undoubtedly disappear if it were not for the army. The army has created the conditions which enable Japan to reap the fruits of the harvest. It has long been our national aim to receive the reward due us for our sacrifices and labors in Manchuria. But what was the Ministry of Foreign Affairs able to do? Diplomacy made concession after concession to China. Our rights and interests were trampled on. Even after the events in Mukden and during the rapid development of military operations, the Ministry of Foreign Affairs sought by every manner of means to put a stop to them, despite the army's firm determination to settle the Manchurian question at once. I am convinced that it would be very dangerous to have trusted our national diplomacy to the Ministry of Foreign Affairs, which is incapable of visualizing our national destinies. The whole nation has by now become convinced that only the army is able to uphold our rights and interests, acquired at the grievous cost of so much money and life, that only the army is able to conduct a national policy. . . .

The army should extract the maximum benefit offered by this situation and convince the nation that weakness of our defences means a direct blow at our national prestige and power. We must make the whole nation understand that it is imperative at least to maintain our present armed forces for defense in order to safeguard our national policy. On the other hand, we must make all political leaders declare their loyalty to the army and navy and introduce a "stronger navy" plank into every party's platform. . . . Unless a firm policy is introduced at the present moment, the army and navy will be constantly menaced with a reduction in armaments as an economy measure and will be in a constant state of uncertainty.

These views were developed and set forth as an official program of the military circles at a conference held in the Ministry of War on July 5, 1932. The conference took up the principal points of government policy, in particular questions of foreign and economic policy and political sentiments in Japan. By decision of the conference the principle of army non-interference in political questions was renounced, on the ground that "the period through which Japan is now passing is so complicated and critical that the army must pay no attention to censure and discard the tradition of non-interference."

In the resolutions of the conference it was pointed out that regular conferences of the Ministry of War must discuss all questions of domestic and foreign policy, Japan's relations with the League of Nations and China as regards the Manchurian question, and relations with all other foreign powers. Decisions on the questions that are capable of execution by the armed forces should be carried out immediately, and the others be passed on by the Minister of War to the Prime Minister with the demand that they be carried out.

In a speech which he delivered at this conference, General Araki declared

The army should be prepared not only for military action but for solving economic, social and cultural problems, pursuing in foreign policy an independent line founded on firm, sound and just premises.

Nor did the decisions of that conference remain mere empty phrases. Only recently the *Miyako* wrote that:

. . . Araki at every meeting of the government presents a new list of demands which make the ministers pale and speechless. . . . It sometimes happens that Araki is the only one to take the floor at these meetings.

On every question the militarists attempt to have the final word.

This hegemony of the militarists is proclaimed as the only sound embodiment of a national policy and is used to rally all the reactionary elements about the army. Thus the army assumes or rather strengthens its rôle as the central nucleus of reaction.

The second point which is the keystone of the whole program of the militarists is

that of creating a "Greater Japan" and the resultant foreign policy.

A person who stood close to the Japanese militarists wrote in 1932, that

. . . the Ministry for Foreign Affairs is almost entirely supported by the Sidehara clique. He had been among the rulers in the Minseito cabinets, in both the Hamaguchi and Wakatsuki cabinets. One need but mention that behind him stands one of the four capitalist concerns, the Mitsubisi, to make it plain that the foreign policy of Sidehara corresponds to those interests. . . . The military authorities were not satisfied with that policy. Following the Mukden incident the dual foreign policy began to give way to the foreign policy of the military circles.

By the "Sidehara policy" the militarists in their agitation mean the excessive cautiousness, shiftiness and willingness to make concessions, allegedly shown by the Minseito group in their dealings with foreign powers in the course of the struggle for the repartitioning of colonies and the subjecting of the colonial peoples. The old party governments are condemned for having signed the Washington agreement, whereby Japan was to evacuate Shantung, and the Kellogg pact, which is unacceptable to Japan inasmuch as it does not provide any clause to cover Japanese interests in Manchuria. In like manner the militarists condemn the London Naval Armaments Pact since this pact assures the superiority of the naval forces of the other imperialist powers as compared with the Japanese.

In opposition to this policy, the militarists propose the armed fist in China and facing the other imperialist powers with the *fait accompli* of increased Japanese influence in new regions and territories. Whereas the Minseito politicians sought to strengthen their hold on Manchuria by bribing the Manchurian generals, the militarist cabinet of General Tanaka sought to attain the same thing by wrecking the train of Chiang Tso-lin. When these attempts failed and Chiang Tso-lin's successor, the "young Marshal" Chiang Hsueh-liang, also adopted a pro-American policy, the militarists arranged the "Nakamura incident" and occupied Manchuria. While the Minseito sought ways and means to have the "Japanese policy in China correctly understood" by the League of Nations and the United States, the militarists consider it more effective for Japan to proceed independently in China. In their agitation the militarists berate "Anglo-Saxon influence," expose "white exploitation of Asia," accuse the British of "enslaving India," and hold it up as Japan's mission to "free the Asiatic peoples by spreading the idea of empire."

In the article, "Problems Facing Japan in the Era of Showa," General Araki writes:

Different countries in Eastern Asia are the objects of oppression on the part of the white race. Awakened Imperial Japan can no longer tolerate the arbitrariness of the white race.

Such are the outward features of disagreement between the militarists and the parliamentary party circles in matters of foreign policy. These outward features are not without objective significance: they actually show the great adventurist spirit of the militarists and the more shifty, uncertain character of the aims of the parliamentary party circles which are connected by sharp factional struggle, by the interests of certain firms, by the fear of the bourgeoisie to lose its foreign markets, foreign credits, etc. Yet the outward appearance of these disagreements does not warrant the formation of any opinion on the significance of these differences as regards the direction which the foreign policy of Japanese imperialism is likely to take in the immediate future.

In a number of cases the parliamentary party groups deliberately emphasized for the benefit of foreigners the independent position of the militarists, sometimes to relieve themselves of the responsibility for the army's too evident aggressiveness (which, however, did not prevent the ruling classes from taking full advantage of the fruits of aggression) but still more often to force the other imperialist powers to make concessions to the Japanese viewpoint, threatening that otherwise the militarists would turn to account the diplomatic defeat of the political parties in order to establish their own complete control, in which case, the politicians argue, the other powers will have to contend with a Japanese viewpoint that is even more intractable. In this connection it is highly significant, for example, that in response to the speech of the American Secretary of State Stimson, on August 8, 1932, blaming Japanese aggression for the events in Manchuria, Japanese government circles declared that the position taken by Stimson "makes it more difficult for the Japanese government to control Japanese public opinion." Immediately "public opinion," the expression of which had been usurped by the militarists and the reactionary-nationalist organizations, gave vent to a number of new attacks upon the government's foreign policy.

Much more clearly does the difference between the militarists and the core of the parliamentary parties, the Minseito in particular, stand out with reference to the question of who the immediate enemy of Japan shall be. As we have already pointed out, the basic questions of Japanese foreign policy are arising at the very moment when the aim of the Manchurian occupation has been achieved, but now the question arises against whom first to wield this weapon. Of course, the militarists also seek to penetrate into the interior of China, and they will use the smallest loophole that occurs in the Far Eastern policy of the United States and the European imperialist powers to extend the sphere of Japanese influence in China.

It is true, that the so-called "fascists" raise the loudest cry of all regarding "white oppression" and American and British betrayal. But at the same time they consider that their principal enemy is the Soviets and that to insure the success of the Japanese-Soviet war which they are preparing, they must come to an understanding with the other imperialist countries. Not long ago Hirata, a well-known military publicist who is a member of a number of reactionary chauvinist organizations, wrote:

We must boldly carry out the principles of realism as during the period of the Meiji government. This military alliance will add to our strength, multiplying it several times over in the period of actual war. The one-time Anglo-Japanese alliance helped to raise the Japanese flag on the continent. Just as the Japanese-Soviet war, in the near future, will be a continuation of the earlier Russo-Japanese war, a new Anglo-Japanese alliance will amount to nothing more than a renewal of the old.

Influential circles of the militarists regard the Soviet Union as their immediate enemy. In their view, Manchuria must serve first and foremost as a drill ground for the war on the Soviets. For this reason, the higher army circles disapproved of the operations which the navy began in Shanghai, and were slow to support it, for they felt that the use of the navy would automatically bring Japan in conflict with the United States and Great Britain, when attention should be principally centered upon war preparations against the Soviet Union. For these groups, Manchuria is but the first link in a chain, the other links of which, in order, will be Jehol and Chahar, then Outer Mongolia, and finally Primorye, the Amur district and Transbaikal. The conflict as they see it is to begin with the seizure of the Chinese-Eastern Railway, then Outer Mongolia and after that "Siberia." With a cynical frankness, Lieutenant-General Kiokatsu Sato speaks of this in his book.

If the Japanese wish with their own hands to exploit Manchuria, Mongolia and Siberia, they must first start by seizing the Chinese-Eastern Railway and the Siberian Railway. Negotiations should be started with the Russian and Chinese governments for the purchase of these roads by Japan at an opportune moment.

For exploiting Mongolia, it is first of all necessary to build a railroad from Mukden to Urga. This road, with its terminus in Mukden, should pass through Tunliaoho, western Liaoho and Little Khingan entering Outer Mongolia. It should then proceed by way of Chachenkhania to Urga. Further on at Irkutsk the road should join the Siberian railway. Should such a railway be built, the mineral resources abounding in the region of Jehol and Chahar and also the Altai plateau, lying to the west of Urga, will be properly exploited. If possible the Mukden-Urga-Irkutsk railroad should be extended from Irkutsk to the north as far as the port of Okhotsk, on the shore of the Okhotsk Sea. Should this plan for the railroad be carried out, practically all Mongolia and a section of Siberia will come within the sphere of Japanese influence.

On this subject, Araki, in the article previously quoted, expressed himself with greater caution. Yet even he does not conceal the contemplated direction of Japanese aggression. He writes:

Japan has no desire to admit the existence of such an ambiguous territory as Mongolia in the immediate vicinity of the Japanese sphere of influence. Mongolia must, at all events, be a territory belonging to the East and it must be given peace and quiet. It cannot be left in the position where other countries spread their aggressive policies with respect to it. To leave Mongolia in its ambiguous position means to maintain a center of disorder in the Far East.

It could be said that the problem of spreading the Imperial idea in Mongolia is more difficult than the same problem with respect to

Manchuria. The thought must here be expressed clearly and frankly that whatever enemy opposes the spread of the Imperial idea must be destroyed.

Though perhaps only a few of the Japanese militarists harbor General Sato's grand schemes of seizing the territory up to the Irkutsk-Okhotsk line, the problem of Outer Mongolia, Primorye and Sakhalin is discussed widely. The belligerent groups of the Japanese militarists emphasize strongly that (when the balance of forces will no longer be in Japan's favor) the Primorye and Sakhalin question must be settled as an organic part of the Greater Japan scheme before 1935–1936. And although by next year the re-equipping of the Japanese army will not yet have been completed, yet the sooner the Japanese army proceeds to settle this question, the better. This is prompted by the consideration that, in the first place, only in that event will the danger of an air attack upon the islands of Japan from the mainland be averted; secondly that the Sea of Japan will thereby become a Japanese inland sea; and thirdly, that the problem of securing oil and coal bases for Japan will thereby have been decisively solved.

Among the Japanese militarists there is further the conviction that while Japanese penetration into Central Asia would lead to a conflict with the United States and Great Britain, a war on the U.S.S.R. would, on the contrary, be greeted with approval by the imperialist powers of the West. Concerning this, the statement made by a former military attaché of the Japanese Embassy in Moscow is typical. At a meeting of officers of the Tokyo garrison in the summer of 1932, he stated that for the U.S.S.R. a war with Japan would mean a simultaneous war on its western borders, and that accordingly the possibilities of assigning Soviet forces for the defense of the Far-Eastern frontiers of the U.S.S.R. would be limited, which increases the vulnerability of these frontiers and of the Siberian railroad trunk lines.

Thus the slogans raised by the Japanese militarists: "Spread the idea of empire among the peoples of Asia!" "Throw off white domination!" "A greater Japan!" "An independent foreign policy for Japan!" etc., are expressions of those adventurist aims which are intended to hasten both the consolidation of Japanese imperialism on the mainland of Asia and the war with this aim, to be directed first and foremost against the U.S.S.R.

Among the questions of internal policy, as we have already said, one of the basic points on the program of the militarists is the demand for increased control of industry and finance by the state. This demand is screened by the slogan of "state capitalism" or "state socialism." There is no need to prove that this slogan arises directly from the interests of the entire *bloc* of the ruling classes in whose hands the state apparatus lies, and that it is not in contradiction to the *ultimate* interests of the capitalists in so far as the realization of this slogan facilitates the success of Japan's imperialist aggression and the suppression of the labor movement in the country; although this realization means cramping the interests of certain groups of the bourgeoisie at some time or other. At the same time this does not prevent the militarists from veiling this slogan with "anti-capitalist" phrases, intended to attract to the militarists the sympathies of the broad intermediate social strata. Araki in his article, "Problems Facing Japan in the Era of Showa," writes:

Capitalists are concerned only with their own interests and pay no attention to public life; politicians often forget the general situation in the country while absorbed in their party interests. . . .

The state presumably stands above class and party interests, defending the interests of the nation as a whole; and therefore the decisive word on all questions touching the life of society must be granted precisely to the state.

This is argued also on the strength of the historical peculiarities of Japan. One Japanese author in expounding the viewpoint of the militarists says:

> The growth of Japanese capitalism has from its very birth been aided by the state and this capitalism at present depends even more on government subsidies than the capitalism of any other country. . . . Today Japanese capitalist interests resemble feudal formations. The militarists think that Japanese capitalism capitulates before the state just as the feudal lords voluntarily surrendered to the state during the "Meiji revolution."

The result of this must be a new order, as the former Japanese Military Attaché in the U.S.S.R., Kasahara, recently stated: "Neither capitalism nor communism, but 'state socialism' is suitable for Japan."

As to how Japan will look under this "state socialism," (*i.e.*, the capitulation of capitalism to the monarchy, which the militarists term the "second restoration" after the first "Meiji restoration"), the militarists prefer to speak less. In the meantime it concretizes this program on two points. The first concerns the "economic *bloc*, of Japan, Korea, Manchuria and Mongolia." The Japanese press, which is under the influence of the militarists, proved daily in 1932 that the rational exploitation of the wealth of Manchuria and Mongolia would be possible only if these countries were not given over to the control of predatory groups of finance capital but would be exploited by the state in a planned manner. This, however, does not exclude private capital investments; but the latter must be made in enterprises jointly with the state.

The Southern Manchurian Railroad which is a semi-government, semi-private enterprise can be pointed to as an example. This very example enables us to judge the "state socialism" of Colonel Kasahara. As is known, the Southern Manchurian Railroad is the arena of activity of one of the largest financial concerns of Japan, the Yasuda Bank, which is the chief private shareholder in the road. The road brings in millions in dividends to finance capital yearly. Its distinction from private enterprise, however, is that the state, *i.e.*, the military police-monarchy, which has at its disposal the controlling parcel of shares of the road, has unrestricted power to use the road for its own needs. Last year particularly we were able to see how the Southern Manchurian Railroad transported vast military supplies free of charge, thus secretly financing the war in Manchuria. This entailed great losses for the small shareholders, whose dividends were drastically cut, but did not injure the situation of the financial monopolies and enriched the War Office. It was precisely because of these operations that the former chairman of the Southern Manchurian Railroad, Uchida, came close to the militarists and was put foward by them as the Minister for Foreign Affairs. The militarists wanted to begin by establishing similar systems in all the other important colonial enterprises. Thus "state socialism" of the type of the Southern Manchurian Railroad or the "economic *bloc* of Japan and Manchuria" means a union of the militarists with finance capital, but the basis of this union must be the concentration of the maximum material resources on the preparation for war, on the financing of war, on the strengthening of the material base of Japanese militarism. It is unnecessary to prove that in the end this represents the expansion of the sphere of activity for these same financial concerns.

Added to this is the demand for "state control of the war industry." It must be borne in mind that the concept "war industry" is a very flexible one, both because of contemporary methods of warfare and the size of present-day armies; no branch of industry exists which will not be militarized to a greater or lesser degree.

"A Lecture on War-time Economics," by Professor Tacso Mori and "Material on General State Mobilization," published in June 1932 by the magazine *Nippon Keizai Nenpo,* are of great interest in understanding this question. Both these documents agree in asserting that

from the moment war is declared we can expect the introduction of "state capitalism." . . . The state will have to take a hand in the production and distribution of all basic products of consumption. In case of necessity the government can declare a monopoly on a number of products of which there is a scarcity. . . . Part of the factories will become the property of the government, part remain in the hands of individuals, but will work under the control of the government, which will undertake to subsidize and supply them with raw materials. . . . Agriculture and trade during the time of war will, of course, also be subjected to government control. . . . The government will perforce have recourse to various compulsory measures for floating internal loans. . . .

This is, so to say, the "maximum program" in time of war, but the "minimum program" is a gradual preparation for this by seizing control of various firms.

Although the speculative "freedom" of the individual capitalist groups is cramped by the system of "state capitalism," still, as the experience of the World War of 1914–1918 has shown, the interests of the capitalist class as a whole benefited from it, and the largest capitalists were able to assure themselves scandalously large profits through furnishing war supplies. And all the Japanese authors who write of "state capitalism" do not forget to stress that the government will not encroach upon the interests of the capitalists and that the organizations set up by finance capital will be used as the basis for the organization of economy in wartime.

The government — says Tacso Mori — controlling all branches of production, naturally cannot concentrate the entire economy of the country in its hands. The people who ran them before the war will remain the owners of the enterprises. The state, by supplying industry with raw materials and receiving from it finished products, effects the necessary control.

The so-called rationalization measures for the unification of industry completely assure the control of industry in war time also; the cartelization and syndicalization of contemporary industry — these are peace-time organizations, fully prepared for the management of industry in time of war.

To an even less degree do the interests of the capitalist class suffer from that "control" which the militarists demand at present. We mean the distribution of profits among the various capitalist groups and grants for the satisfaction of either present or future needs connected with the war. This is very evident in the example of the "economic *bloc* of Japan and Manchuria," cited above. One of the problems precipitating the raising of the question of an "economic bloc" was the import into Japan of Manchurian coal, dug in the Fushun coal mines belonging to the Southern Manchurian Railroad. Japanese coal companies demanded a restriction of this import in order to maintain the price of coal on the Japanese market at a high level. If they talked of the "interests of the nation," these solicitations should, of course, have been rejected. Actually, however, neither the civil part of the government nor the military went further than a dispute as to the percentage by which it was necessary to cut the import of Fushun coal. Consequently they talked of the division of profits between the Japanese coal companies and the shareholders of the Southern Manchurian Railroad, in the development of which the military clique was especially interested. At present the problem of the entire industrial construction in Manchuria is put on the same plane as the question of curtailing the import of Korean rice into Japan for the purpose of settling the dispute between the Japanese and Korean landowners and rice-trading firms.

Thus, the "state capitalism" (or "state socialism") of General Araki is not only not opposed to capitalism and the monopolies of finance capital, but for two reasons strengthens them. First, because it brings the state apparatus still closer to the organizations of finance capital and therefore allows the latter even more unceremoniously to dip into the pocket of the state, as was done up to the present in Japan (it is necessary to add, moreover, that Japanese financiers surpassed their colleagues throughout the world in the use of state subsidies, state orders, etc.). Secondly, the situation of finance capital is strengthened thanks to the fact that "state control" means a strengthening of the monarchy, which is the bulwark of the most reactionary and most aggressive elements in the country, *i.e.*, strengthening the possibility of further pressure on the working class (in particular — by means of militarizing the most important enterprises), more favorable conditions for conquering new colonial markets, etc. Finance capital, therefore, had no cause to fear the "second restoration" of General Araki. And if financial concerns reject this slogan, it is not because they really believe in the possibility of some super-class "state socialism" which will somehow be effected after the "second restoration," but because not a single group of the Japanese bourgeoisie to-day is willing to yield its profits, the opportunity of free commercial and financial operations and the opportunity of shifting the losses caused by the crisis onto the non-monopoly groups of the bourgeoisie, onto agriculture, the consuming masses, tax-payers and even onto each other (onto the very monopolists, in the course of the competitive war between them). To an even less degree are the financial concerns

prepared to allow General Araki himself to determine that share of the profits of the bourgeoisie which must go in payment of military expenses. The bourgeoisie of Japan is prepared to shoulder very big war expenditures; it knows that these expenditures will be redeemed, but it wants to determine for itself how much of its own money it can give for this purpose, *i.e.*, to be master in its own enterprises and master of its own money. By no means does it want to grant the decision of this question to the semi-feudal military clique.

The second point on the program of the Japanese militarists in questions of internal policy is bound up with the bitter intensification of the agrarian crisis. The leaders of the militarists cannot ignore this issue; first, because they themselves and a very large number of the young officers come from the ranks of the middle and petty landowners, whose profits have been drastically cut by the fall in prices of agricultural products and by the necessity of paying ever increasing interest on debts to mortgage-banks and whose very existence is threatened by the ever increasing antilandowners' movement of the tenant-peasantry. Secondly, the militarists cannot evade this issue because the vast majority of Japanese soldiers are peasants and the catastrophic speed with which the ruin of the peasant masses is progressing and the growth of their social discontent threaten to create very big political difficulties within the army itself, to undermine its fighting capacity, to disorganize such an important tool of the militarists as the Society of Reservists, the majority of whom are peasants.

The sharpening of the agrarian crisis in the summer of 1932 as a result of the fall in the price of silk, coming together with the crop failure and famine in the northern prefectures, and with the flow into the country of unemployed workers forced out of the cities by the industrial crisis, compelled the militarists to pay special attention to the situation on the countryside. Even for those strata of the militarists not directly connected with the landowners, the sharpening of this question was advantageous, since it allowed them on the one hand to win for the army the sympathy of a considerable part of the reactionary nationalist movement, and, on the other, to divert from revolutionary organizations the peasant masses awakening to active struggle. Thus during the spring and early summer of 1932 there was formed the "united front" of the Araki group — the Society of Reservists, the Imperial Agricultural Society (an organization of landowners), agrarian deputies in parliament and a number of reactionary-nationalist organizations — with the purpose of securing government measures to "aid agriculture." Through the efforts of this *bloc* a colossal agitation campaign was developed. The newspapers published innumerable articles on the agrarian crisis. With the aid of the Society of Reservists peasant signatures were collected on the countryside for petitions to the government to aid agriculture, and special peasant delegations went to Tokyo with these petitions. Tens and hundreds of various projects were proposed to "aid the country."

All these projects have one thing in common: not one of them contains anything regarding actual aid to the toiling peasantry and the substance of the noisy campaign for "saving the country" is a demand for government aid to the landowning kulak upper strata of the countryside. This is first of all shown by the fact that not one of the numerous projects for aiding the country (with the exception of the demagogic platform of the centrist *Rono Tai-Siuto*) included a demand for a cancellation or decrease of or a moratorium on tenant payments. In general, all the projects demand the purchase by the government of rice and of silk cocoons, which is of advantage first of all to the landowners. They demand the extension of government credits on real estate, the curtailment of the import of Korean and Formosan rice into Japan, government aid to the local banks on operations for the purchase of agrarian estates, etc. The political ideology, landowning in substance, of those who led this campaign is self-evident.

Soon, however, General Araki had to do without the wide support given him by this movement in the beginning. The point is that the government policy of aid to agriculture called forth opposition from the powerful industrial bourgeoisie which was not connected with the village. The industrialists themselves lay claim to maximum state aid. With the purpose of getting subsidies the Central Association of Industrial Societies inaugurated a wide campaign for assistance to the petty and middle industrialists and organized a corresponding petition movement, carried on agitation in the press, etc. This action signalized the determination of the industrial bourgeoisie to fight for its share of plunder of the government funds and, therefore, its interests clashed with those of the agrarians and merchant exporters. The struggle for the utilization of the state funds reached such a point that the militarists, with Araki at the head, now favored a maximum curtailment of the plans for financial aid.

As early as July 1, 1932, General Araki pointed out in his "four points of advice to the Premier" that military circles see as the most important task of the day the solution of the Manchurian problems and that in overcoming the agricultural crisis it is necessary "to increase the independence of the countryside." At the end of July, Araki stated at a conference of governors:

I completely approve of the necessity of salutary measures in connection with the economic crisis, but it should not be forgotten for a moment that the settling of the Manchurian-Mongolian problem is of greatest importance.

Such statements made it clear that the militarists did not agree to the unlimited squandering of state funds on the agrarians and industrialists, and that state subsidies must first of all be directed towards preparation for war.

In the autumn of 1932, in a special article published in *Chuo Koron,* General Araki developed his views on the situation of the countryside and measures for improving it. We shall say a few words about this article, which shows with unusual clarity what sort of "friend of the peasantry" the militarist is. General Araki admits that the crisis is felt with particular severity by the peasantry, as well as by all intermediate strata of the country and city:

The peasants, petty traders and owners of enterprises — he writes — have been drained to such a degree that they cannot resume their former activity no matter how much they may try.

What is the cause of this "draining of the peasantry"? It appears that it is not the landowners' exploitation, not the sapping of the countryside by trade and finance capital, not the burden of state taxes and not the backwardness of Japanese agriculture with its technical stagnation resulting from the above-mentioned reasons, and the indebtedness, impoverishment and pauperization of the peasantry. Araki did not say one word about these things; deliberately and consciously, he was silent about them.

Moreover, he pictured the matter in such a way as to make it appear that Japanese agriculture had made tremendous strides forward in its technical development and all its trouble consisted in the peasants being freed from a large part of their work by the machine (a thing as rare in the Japanese rural districts as in the Indian and Chinese countryside) and giving themselves up to idleness.

Look at the work of the peasants at the present time — says General Araki — there is widespread modernization and mechanization of implements. Irrigation of the fields and of other tilled lands which was formerly done by treadmills (turned by the weight of a person) is now done by a pump with an electric motor. A turn of a pointer will do all the heavy work. Formerly the peasants went on foot over their fields, now they ride on bicycles. Time and labor are saved. But on what do they spend this time and labor? On nothing at all. They waste time and energy, which formerly was spent on useful work, to no purpose at all. What they lack is the firmness and resolution to struggle with the crisis.

Well, since the peasantry is itself to blame for its disastrous plight, it must not ask for aid. It must discard all hopes for financial aid from the government. The only aid which would be desirable for the government to give would be assistance in organizing various coöperative enterprises among the peasants, who thus could use their labor for their own benefit.

Such aid as money grants without any definite aim — writes General Araki — is not a means of saving the peasants at the present time when the crisis has deeply affected the entire economic life of the country. If money were given, they would immediately spend it and again be in the same difficult situation tomorrow. The word "aid" is not necessary at the present time. A better term would be "coöperation." Give them work on coöperative enterprises.

And Araki relates how a certain major-general increased the well-being of the peasants in a village near Kumamoto by forcing them to cultivate vegetables for the market and twist straw into ropes for sale. The advice of Araki:

. . . mutual aid among the peasants, small traders and owners of small enterprises. Capital for beginning the work, and leadership — that is the necessity at the present moment when poverty is widely spread among the people.

This "benevolent" advice is given to the peasantry when the government, even after all curtailments, yearly spends hundreds of millions of yen, drained from the peasantry by taxation, on aiding the landowners. The class interests of the militarists render them completely unable to show the peasant masses any way out of the crisis, in spite of the fact that the militarists realize all the danger of the growth of dissatisfaction among the peasant sections of the army and at first tried to avert it.

Finally, the last point of the domestic political program of the militarists, and one which does not demand any special clarification, is the suppression of the revolutionary movement within the country. In practice the militarists concentrate their attention on this point of internal policy. The trite argument advanced in mass agitation in favor of this idea is that the unity of the whole nation is the first condition for finding a way out of the crisis. General Araki writes in one of his numerous articles:

Japan is at the present moment confronted with a crisis. She is like a small vessel which struggles with the tumultuous waves of a stormy ocean. . . . Here there is no place for the question: who are the captain, the officers, the crew or the passengers? — all must help. In order to surmount the difficulties in the way, everybody, rich and poor, peasants and workers, young and old, men and women, all must unite for one purpose — to overcome the crisis. The difficulties connected with the Manchurian question and with the League of Nations, the internal economic difficulties, the differences among the people — all this will be solved at once, if the whole people will strive for it.

"To solve at once" in the mouth of General Araki, means to choose the path of war and for this it is necessary first to smash the only genuine adversary of a new imperialist war: the Communist movement within Japan itself. Of course they do not stop at anti-Communist speeches and articles. Thousands of Communists arrested in 1932, a whole series of measures instituted for increasing and strengthening the police and gendarme apparatus, the smashing of all Left organizations which could be used by the Communists as a legal cover, and of all revolutionary trade unions, the arrest of hundreds of intellectuals suspected of giving material aid to the Communist Party, the suppression by arms of workers' strikes and peasant conflicts — this is all part of the plan of "uniting the nation." But these measures must be supplemented by others in order to achieve their purpose: by attempts with the help of social demagogy and chauvinist intoxication disseminated by reactionary-chauvinist organizations to distract the masses from the revolutionary path to which they are impelled by the intensification of the crisis. Hence, we have wide support by the leaders of the militarists not only of those reactionary chauvinist organizations which unite social strata homogeneous with the upper crust of the militarists (for example, the Society of the Foundations of the State) or which wholly depend on the militarists (for example, the Society of the Black Dragon) but also of organizations of the reactionary petty bourgeoisie which specialize in capitalist demagogy, at the same time pointing a way out of the crisis to the masses not through revolution but through imperialist aggression and a return to the past — to the epoch of absolute monarchy and military dictatorship (for example, all the organizations of S. Okawa and Ikki Kita) and even the "national-socialist" organizations (Michikawa, Simonaka, Akamatsu).

The necessity for the political organizations of the militarists to use a certain amount of social demagogy in the struggle against the revolutionary movement arises from the fact already mentioned that the spirit of social discontent is pentrating not only the masses of the soldiers and the rank and file of the Society of Reservists but even the ranks of the young officers. Therefore the militarist leaders must cloak their reactionary and aggressive plans in the language of patriotic love for the people. A vivid example of this is the agitation of the officers' organizations on the eventful day of May 15, 1932. In one of the leaflets issued on this day by the National Federation of Young Officers, we read:

The Japanese army and navy, true to their Emperor, sympathize with the people, who are unjustly injured by cheap politicians and parliamentarians who have sold themselves for money, and by lovers of easy profits. The Japanese army and navy, bound body and soul to the people, to the traditions of *Busido,* see with indignation the influence of commercial, speculative circles growing to the detriment of national patriotism. The army and navy will come to the aid of the people.

In another leaflet, published on the same day, May 15, the young officers wrote:

Japanese nation! In the name of the Emperor, destroy the existing political parties which are the common enemy of the nation. Kill the capitalists, punish the arbitrary authorities, kill the sly landowners and the special privileged class. Peasants, workers and the whole nation, defend yourselves and guard your fatherland. Under the leadership of our able and august Emperor, we must restore the true soul of our empire. We must institute the principle of self-government. It is necessary to draw in capable people. Complete destruction is necessary for great reconstruction. We mourn the present situation in Japan. . . . We need not say that we are neither socialists nor extreme nationalists. Arise, people, and restore fallen Japan!

All this demagogy, of course, does not change the fact that the core of the real program of the militarists remains the struggle for strengthening the basis of the military-police monarchy as the support of everything reactionary within the country and the struggle for accelerating the expansion of Japanese military-feudal imperialism. But this demagogy helps the leaders of the militarists to attract ever-wider social strata to the support of their program, actually increasing the social base of the monarchy.

It is extremely doubtful whether the militarist leaders can by these means attain permanent success among the peasant masses (even among the majority of the peasant owners) and among the lower strata of the urban petty bourgeoisie. At the same time considerable reactionary forces can be established for a certain period of time among the petty bourgeoisie in the town and country and of course among the landowners. In the course of 1932 the Araki group succeeded in rallying to itself the young officers, who are now inclined to obey only Araki and not the government.

The essence of the Japanese army — recently wrote the magazine *Chuo Koron* — lies in the fact that as an army of the Emperor it carries out the tasks of peace, not taking orders from the government and not being subject to parliament.

The author of this article notes with satisfaction that the young officers, instead of obeying the government, choose to obey Araki:

Among the young officers, up to the rank of staff-officers, there exists a special movement of "Araki-ists," who treat Araki as a god.

In the first half of 1932, when there was a very tense economic and political situation in Japan and when her external political relations, especially in connection with the defeats in China, were exceedingly strained, the militarists succeeded in using all the levers of the reactionary-chauvinist movement. Just in this period the militarists became the center, around which, directly or indirectly, gathered all the reactionary-chauvinist organizations, including the "national-socialists."

II. FASCISM

THE POLITICAL DEVELOPMENTS IN THE 1930'S IN JAPAN REPRESENT A VARIANT OF THE FASCIST MOVEMENTS IN EUROPE BETWEEN THE TWO WORLD WARS.

Plan for the Reorganization of Japan

KITA IKKI

Kita Ikki has been widely regarded as the intellectual mentor of the "fascist" movement in Japan. In what way do his views resemble those of European fascists? How are they specifically Japanese in tone and in content?

At present the Japanese empire is faced with a national crisis unparalleled in its history; it faces dilemmas at home and abroad. The vast majority of the people feel insecure in their livelihood and they are on the point of taking a lesson from the collapse of European societies, while those who monopolize political, military, and economic power simply hide themselves and, quaking with fear, try to maintain their unjust position. Abroad, neither England, America, Germany, nor Russia has kept its word, and even our neighbor China, which long benefited from the protection we provided through the Russo-Japanese War, not only has failed to repay us but instead despises us. Truly we are a small island, completely isolated in the Eastern Sea. One false step and our nation will again fall into the desperate state of crisis — dilemmas at home and abroad — that marked the period before and after the Meiji Restoration.

The only thing that brightens the picture is the sixty million fellow countrymen with whom we are blessed. The Japanese people must develop a profound awareness of the great cause of national existence and of the people's equal rights, and they need an unerring, discriminating grasp of the complexities of domestic and foreign thought. The Great War in Europe was, like Noah's flood, Heaven's punishment on them for arrogant and rebellious ways. It is of course natural that we cannot look to the Europeans, who are out of their minds because of the great destruction, for a completely detailed set of plans. But in contrast Japan, during those five years of destruction, was

From Kita Ikki, *Nihon Kaizō Hōan*, pp. 6–14, in Ryusaku Tsunoda, Wm. Theodore de Bary, and Donald Keene, compilers, *Sources of the Japanese Tradition*, pp. 775–84 (New York: Columbia University Press, 1958).

blessed with five years of fulfillment. Europe needs to talk about reconstruction, while Japan must move on to reorganization. The entire Japanese people, thinking calmly from this perspective which is the result of Heaven's rewards and punishments, should, in planning how the great Japanese empire should be reorganized, petition for a manifestation of the imperial prerogative establishing "a national opinion in which no dissenting voice is heard, by the organization of a great union of the Japanese people." Thus, by homage to the emperor, a basis for national reorganization can be set up.

Truly, our seven hundred million brothers in China and India have no path to independence other than that offered by our guidance and protection. And for our Japan, whose population has doubled within the past fifty years, great areas adequate to support a population of at least two hundred and forty or fifty millions will be absolutely necessary a hundred years from now. For a nation, one hundred years are like a hundred days for an individual. How can those who are anxious about these inevitable developments, or who grieve over the desperate conditions of neighboring countries, find their solace in the effeminate pacifism of doctrinaire socialism? I do not necessarily rule out social progress by means of the class struggle. But still, just what kind of so-called science is it that can close its eyes to the competition between peoples and nations which has taken place throughout the entire history of mankind? At a time when the authorities in the European and American revolutionary creeds have found it completely impossible to arrive at an understanding of the "gospel of the sword" because of their superficial philosophy, the noble Greece of Asian culture must complete her national reorganization on the basis of her own national polity. At the same time, let her lift the virtuous banner of an Asian league and take the leadership in a world federation which must come. In so doing let her proclaim to the world the Way of Heaven in which all are children of Buddha, and let her set the example which the world must follow. So the ideas of people like those who oppose arming the nation are after all simply childish.

SECTION ONE: THE PEOPLE'S EMPEROR

Suspension of the Constitution. In order for the emperor and the entire Japanese people to establish a secure base for the national reorganization, the emperor will, by a show of his imperial prerogative, suspend the Constitution for a period of three years, dissolve both houses of the Diet, and place the entire nation under martial law.

(Note 1: In extraordinary times the authorities should of course ignore harmful opinions and votes. To regard any sort of constitution or parliament as an absolute authority is to act in direct imitation of the English and American semisacred "democracy." Those who do so are the obstinate conservatives who hide the real meaning of "democracy"; they are as ridiculous as those who try to argue national polity on the basis of the [Shintō mythological] High Plain of Heaven. . . . The effect of government by votes which has prevailed hitherto is really nothing more than a maintenance of the traditional order; it puts absolute emphasis on numbers and ignores those who would put a premium on quality.)

(Note 2: Those who look upon a *coup d'état* as an abuse of power on behalf of a conservative autocracy ignore history. Napoleon's *coup d'état* in refusing to cooperate with reactionary elements offered the only out for the Revolution at a time when the parliament and the press were alive with royalist elements. And even though one sees in the Russian Revolution an incident in which Lenin dissolved with machine guns a parliament filled with obstructionists, the popular view is still that a *coup d'état* is a reactionary act.)

(Note 3: A *coup d'état* should be looked upon as a direct manifestation of the authority of the nation; that is, of the will of society. The progressive leaders have all arisen from popular groups. They arise because of political leaders like Napoleon and Lenin. In the reorganization of Japan there must be a manifestation of the power inherent in a coalition of the people and sovereign.)

(Note 4: The reason why the Diet must be dissolved is that the nobility and the wealthy upon whom it depends are incapable of standing with the emperor and the people in the cause of reorganization. The necessity for suspension of the Constitution is that these people seek protection in the law codes enacted under it. The reason martial law must be proclaimed is that it is essential for the freedom of the nation that there be no restraint in suppressing the opposition which will come from the above groups.

However, it will also be necessary to suppress those who propagate a senseless and half-understood translation of outside revolutionary creeds as the agents of reorganization.)

The True Significance of the Emperor. The fundamental doctrine of the emperor as representative of the people and as pillar of the nation must be made clear.

In order to clarify this a sweeping reform of the imperial court in the spirit of the Emperor Jimmu in founding the state and in the spirit of the great Meiji emperor will be carried out. The present Privy Councillors and other officials will be dismissed from their posts, and in their place will come talent, sought throughout the realm, capable of assisting the emperor.

A Consultative Council will be established to assist the emperor. Its members, fifty in number, will be appointed by the emperor.

A member of the Consultative Council must tender his resignation to the emperor whenever the cabinet takes action against him or whenever the Diet passes a vote of nonconfidence against him. However, the council members are by no means responsible to either the cabinet or to the Diet. . . .

(Note 2: There is no scientific basis whatever for the belief of the democracies that a state which is governed by representatives voted in by the electorate is superior to a state which has a system of government by a particular person. Every nation has its own national spirit and history. It cannot be maintained, as advocates of this theory would have it, that China during the first eight years of the republic was more rational than Belgium, which retained rule by a single person. The "democracy" of the Americans derives from the very unsophisticated theory of the time which held that society came into being through a voluntary contract based upon the free will of individuals; these people, emigrating from each European country as individuals, established communities and built a country. But their theory of the divine right of voters is a half-witted philosophy which arose in opposition to the theory of the divine right of kings at that time. Now Japan certainly was not founded in this way, and there has never been a period in which Japan was dominated by a half-witted philosophy. Suffice it to say that the system whereby the head of state has to struggle for election by a long-winded self-advertisement and by exposing himself to ridicule like a low-class actor seems a very strange custom to the Japanese people, who have been brought up in the belief that silence is golden and that modesty is a virtue.) . . .

(Note 4: The provision for censure of members of the Consultative Council by cabinet and Diet is required in view of the present situation in which many men do as they wish on the excuse that they are duty-bound to help the Emperor. The obstinacy and arrogance of the members of the Privy Council is not very different from that of the court officials in Russia before the revolution. The men who cause trouble for the emperor are men of this kind.)

The Abolition of the Peerage System. The peerage system will be abolished, and the spirit of the Meiji Restoration will be clarified by removal of this barrier which has come between the emperor and the people.

The House of Peers will be abolished and replaced by a Council of Deliberation, which shall consider action taken by the House of Representatives.

The Council of Deliberation will be empowered to reject decisions taken by the House of Representatives a single time. The members of the Council of Deliberation will consist of distinguished men in many fields of activity, elected by each other and appointed by the emperor. . . .

Universal Suffrage. All men twenty-five years of age, by their rights as people of Great Japan, will have the right, freely and equally, to stand for election to and to vote for the House of Representatives. The same will hold for local self-government assemblies.

Women will not have the right to participate in politics.

(Note 1: Although a tax qualification has determined suffrage in other countries and this system was first initiated in England, where the Parliament was originally set up to supervise the use of tax money collected by the Crown, in Japan we must establish it as a fundamental principle that suffrage is the innate right of the people. This universal suffrage must not be interpreted as a lowering of the tax qualification on grounds that all men pay at least indirect taxes. Rather, suffrage is a "duty of the people" in the same sense that military service is a "duty of the people.")

(Note 2: The duty of the people to defend the country cannot be separated from their duty to participate in its government. As this is a fundamental human right of the Japanese people, there is no reason why the Japanese should be like the slaves in the Roman Empire or like the menials driven from the imperial gate during the monarchical age — simply ruled, having to live and die under orders from a ruling class. Nothing can infringe upon the right and duty of suffrage under any circumstances. Therefore officers and soldiers on active service, even if they are overseas, should elect and be elected without any restrictions.)

(Note 3: The reason for the clear statement that "Women will not have the right to participate in politics" is not that Japanese women today have not yet awakened. Whereas the code of chivalry for knights in medieval Europe called for honoring women and gaining their favor, in medieval Japan the samurai esteemed and valued the person of woman on approximately the same level as they did themselves, while it became the accepted code for women to honor the men and gain their favor. This complete contrast in developments has penetrated into all society and livelihood, and continues into modern history — there has been agitation by women for suffrage abroad while here women have continued devoted to the task of being good wives and wise mothers. Politics is a small part of human activity. The question of the place of women in Japan will be satisfactorily solved if we make an institutional reorganization which will guarantee the protection of woman's right to be "mother of the nation and wife of the nation." To make women accustomed to verbal warfare is to do violence to their natural aptitude; it is more terrible than using them in the line of battle. Anyone who has observed the stupid talkativeness of Western women or the piercing quarrels among

Chinese women will be thankful that Japanese women have continued on the right path. Those who have developed good 'trends should let others who have developed bad trends learn from them. For this reason, one speaks today of a time of fusion of Eastern and Western civilization. But the ugliness of direct and uncritical borrowing can be seen very well in the matter of woman suffrage.)

The Restoration of the People's Freedom. The various laws which have restricted the freedom of the people and impaired the spirit of the constitution in the past — the Civil Service Appointment Ordinance, the Peace Preservation police law, the Press Act, the Publication Law, and similar measures — will be abolished.

(Note: This is obviously right. These laws work only to maintain all sorts of cliques.)

The National Reorganization Cabinet. A Reorganization Cabinet will be organized while martial law is in effect; in addition to the present ministries, it will have ministries for industries and several Ministers of State without Portfolio. Members of the Reorganization Cabinet will not be chosen from the present military, bureaucratic, financial, and party cliques, but this task will be given to outstanding individuals selected throughout the whole country.

All the present prefectural governors will be dismissed from their offices, and National Reorganization Governors will be appointed by the same method of selection as given above.

(Note: This is necessary for the same reasons that the Meiji Revolution could not have been carried out by the Tokugawa shogun and his vassals. But a revolution cannot necessarily be evaluated according to the amount of bloodshed. It is just as impossible to say of a surgical operation that it was not thorough because of the small amount of blood that was lost. It all depends on the skill of the surgeon and

the constitution of the patient undergoing the operation. Japan today is like a man in his prime and in good health. Countries like Russia and China are like old patients whose bodies are in total decay. Therefore, if there is a technician who takes a far-sighted view of the past and present, and who draws judiciously on East and West, the reorganization of Japan can be accomplished during a pleasant talk.)

The National Reorganization Diet. The National Reorganization Diet, elected in a general election and convened during the period of martial law, will deliberate on measures for reorganization.

The National Reorganization Diet will not have the right to deliberate on the basic policy of national reorganization proclaimed by the emperor.

(Note 1: Since in this way the people will become the main force and the emperor the commander, this *coup d'état* will not be an abuse of power but the expression of the national determination by the emperor and the people.)

(Note 2: This is not a problem of legal philosophy but a question of realism; it is not an academic argument as to whether or not the emperors of Russia and Germany were also empowered with such authority, but it is a divine confidence which the people place only in the Emperor of Japan.)

(Note 3: If a general election were to be held in our present society of omnipotent capital and absolutist bureaucracy the majority of the men elected to the Diet would either be opposed to the reorganization or would receive their election expenses from men opposed to the reorganization. But, since the general election will be held and the Diet convened under martial law, it will of course be possible to curb the rights of harmful candidates and representatives.)

(Note 4: It is only because there was such a divine emperor that, despite the fact that the Restoration Revolution was carried out with greater thoroughness than the

French Revolution, there was no misery and disorder. And thanks to the existence of such a godlike emperor, Japan's national reorganization will be accomplished a second time in an orderly manner, avoiding both the massacres and violence of the Russian Revolution and the snail's pace of the German revolution.)

The Renunciation of the Imperial Estate.[1] The emperor will personally show the way by granting the lands, forests, shares, and similar property owned by the Imperial House to the nation.

---

[1] This section was censored in pre-war editions.

The expenses of the Imperial Household will be limited to approximately thirty million yen per year, to be supplied by the national treasury.

However, this amount can be increased with consent of the Diet if the situation warrants such action.

(Note: The present imperial estate began with holdings taken over from the Tokugawa family, and however the true meaning of the emperor might shine forth, it is inconsistent to operate such medieval finances. It is self evident that every expense of the people's emperor should be borne by the nation.)

Can the Reactionary-Chauvinist Movement in Japan Be Called Fascist?

KARL RADEK

One of the most detailed treatments of Japanese "fascism" was written by Tanin and Yohan and, rather surprisingly, comes to the conclusion that the "reactionary chauvinist movement," as they call it, was *not* fascist in the West European sense of the word. This thesis is energetically attacked by another Marxist writer, Karl Radek, who was soon to succumb in the Russian purges. Radek uses his introduction to the book as the place to demolish one of its principal theses.

Inasmuch as all three writers share the same fundamental political-economic philosophy, we can expect them to agree on their definition of fascism. Where Radek differs from Tanin and Yohan is in the application of this definition to the case of Japan. It would require a detailed knowledge of pre-war Japan to determine how far Radek's critique is correct. His introductory essay does, however, point up some of the difficulties we are bound to confront in answering the question of whether or not Japan ever actually became a fascist state.

I SHALL . . . confine myself to one question put by the authors in the last chapter of their work, the question *of the resemblance and differences between Japanese and European fascism,* a question of great import for the appraisal of the perspectives of development in the Far East. . . .

The authors ask: "Can this whole reactionary chauvinist movement . . . be called 'fascist' in the West European sense of the word?" They answer this question in the negative, and they advance the following reason for their negative answer: ". . . if we investigate it [this movement] as a whole we find that it is characterized by two distinct traits in which it differs from, say, Italian or German fascism."

What are those distinct features?

The first difference amounts to this — that West European fascism is primarily an instrument of finance capital, while the Japanese reactionary chauvinist movement, taken as a whole, is the instrument not only of finance capital but also of the Japanese monarchy which represents a *bloc* of two class forces: finance capital and semi-feudal landowners, and besides this possesses the logic of its own development, represented by the army and monarchist bureaucracy whose oppression has an independent significance. That is why at the center of the Japanese reactionary chauvinist movement we find principally the same people who head the system of Japanese military-feudal imperialism. Hence, the rôle of the army as the backbone of the reactionary chauvinist movement taken as a whole.

The second distinguishing trait of the Japanese reactionary chauvinist movement, char-

From the introduction by Karl Radek to *Militarism and Fascism in Japan* by O. Tanin and E. Yohan (New York: International Publishers, 1934), pp. 7–22.

acteristic of the most important and so far the most influential wing of it, follows from this. It is the limited use of social demagogy by the reactionary chauvinist movement as a whole.

Before we put this motivation to an analysis, it is necessary to point out that only such phenomena may be compared with each other which have resemblance as well as points of difference. Phenomena having no resemblance cannot be compared at all. It is therefore methodologically wrong when the authors speak only of the distinctions between the military-fascist movement in Japan and European fascism, and say nothing about their resemblance, although the very term "military-fascist movement" indicates that they do see this resemblance. The failure to analyze the features of resemblance inevitably leads to one-sidedness which Lenin often called an "exaggeration of the truth."

Fascism is a phase in the development of monopoly capitalism at a certain stage in its decay, disintegration, crisis. Wherever monopoly capitalism was victorious it created a tendency to replace democracy, the hidden form of the dictatorship of big capital, by its more or less open forms. From the very moment of the rise of modern imperialism there were tendencies indicated in its policy which, as long ago as the end of the nineteenth and the beginning of the twentieth century, made it possible to talk about the crisis of democracy. Not only the representatives of the revolutionary proletariat, not only the representatives of petty-bourgeois opposition and rebellious currents — anarchists and syndicalists — spoke of this crisis, it was noted also by the representatives of feudal and semi-feudal reaction (*cf.* the literature of French royalists, of the German reactionary groups as, for instance, Delbruck), it was noticed by business men, who described the growing power of the finance oligarchy. The literature dealing with American internal politics at the end of the nineteenth

and the beginning of the twentieth century abounds in works revealing the decay of bourgeois democracy.

The concentration of power in the hands of capitalist monopolies, trusts and cartels had led even before the war to a state where the decision on all basic questions of policy passed over from the government to uncontrolled, closed capitalist cliques, which influenced the government not through parliamentary channels, but by direct corruption, by the power within the bourgeois parties being transferred to small groups financing these parties and dictating their will to them. All these processes led not only to the weakening of parliamentary democracy, but to the actual curtailing of all so-called rights and liberties, without which bourgeois democracy would be unthinkable. Constant attacks upon the freedom of workers' organizations, upon the right of assembly, freedom of speech, etc., had taken place in the pre-war years[1] in a number of capitalist countries, turning bourgeois democracy more and more into an empty shell, its contents removed.

This process continued at an accelerated tempo during the war, because the war had accentuated the class conflicts to such an extent that the bourgeoisie doubted whether it would be able to realize its aims by way of democracy at all. The military régime did not remove parliamentarism in the leading capitalist countries. Even in the most democratic countries, as, for instance, France, democracy became a means by which the most energetic imperialist cliques came to power (Clemenceau in France), but the "lower" base of bourgeois democracy was disappearing to a considerable extent. Democratic liberties were taken away immediately from proletarian groups *protesting against the imperialist war*. Even petty-bourgeois groups and Social-Democracy, which sided with imperialism, did not

[1] *I.e.* before 1914. [Editor's note]

escape the same lot. The Second International represented the situation as a matter of only a temporary sacrifice, a temporary surrender of democratic liberties, dictated by higher considerations — "Defense of the Fatherland." They asserted that after the war, the proletariat, as a reward for saving the fatherland, would be given an abundance of rights. They were even convinced that, together with this expected abundance of rights, a new era of social reforms would set in.

The years immediately following the world imperialist war, confirmed, as it seemed, these assumptions. They led to the expansion of women's suffrage in England, to the downfall of the empires of the Hohenzollerns and the Hapsburgs, to the creation of republics in the whole of central Europe and in a considerable part of eastern Europe, to the introduction of the eight-hour day and social insurance on a scale unknown before. In a number of countries, including even England, the parties of the Second International came to power. But even at that time this apparent growth of democracy in the countries where capitalism, fearing the proletarian revolution, was putting on democratic airs, was accompanied by violent suppression of the revolutionary movement and of the class organizations of the proletariat. If, in the pre-war period, monopoly capitalism, while emptying the shell of parliamentarism of its contents, outwardly left all the democratic rights of the workers intact (only curtailing them), the bourgeoisie now, with the power of monopoly capitalism constantly increasing behind the scenes, recognized the democratic rights only for those sections of the people which followed the parties supporting its rule. Bourgeois democracy became a democracy for slave-owners and for obedient slaves.

The rise to power of Italian fascism in 1922 marks a certain boundary line in the history of the decay of bourgeois democracy. Italian fascism outlawed not only the revolutionary, but also the reformist sections of the working class, and later even liquidated *Populare,* the reactionary petty-bourgeois party. It has openly abolished all the institutions of bourgeois democracy: parliament, the legal existence of bourgeois political parties, and all the principal democratic rights. Hurriedly waving aside and casting off all vestiges of syndicalist and socialist phrases, Italian fascism, using socialist criticism of liberalism, free competition and capitalist monopoly, has created the theory of the corporate state which, in practice, only covers up the rule of private capitalist organizations, slightly disguised as organs of state capitalist control. The victory of Italian fascism signified that the ruling sections of the bourgeoisie — from the landlords to the big bankers — no longer found it possible to retain power with bourgeois democracy in existence. The right to agitate and organize, which bourgeois democracy had formerly granted to the masses of the people, began to threaten the very existence of monopoly capitalism in those countries where conditions for the development of capitalism were most unstable. The seizure of factories by Italian workers in 1920 had been correctly interpreted by the Italian bourgeoisie as the approach of the proletarian revolution. It found itself helpless in the face of this movement. . . . The bourgeoisie was saved then by the reformist-centrist leadership of the Italian Socialist Party, which had disorganized the entire movement. But the bourgeoisie understood too well that the consequence of the betrayal of the working class by the centrists and reformists would be the shifting of the working masses towards communism, the crystallization of a true revolutionary leadership which would secure victory during the next offensive of the working class. Therefore, the bourgeoisie decided to remove this danger once and for all by abolishing the entire democratic system, setting up an organization strong enough to safeguard capitalism from new dangers. This could not be the narrow organization of the conservative groups, as this organization would have met vehement resistance on the part of the workers and peasants, and could not have obtained any other support except that of the army and the police. The new counter-revolutionary organization had to be a mass organization, as its task was to fight the mass revolutionary movement. In order to become a mass organization, it had to make its appearance under a pseudo-revolutionary banner, use the slogans of social demagogy, and thus divert the social discontent of the backward vacillating masses away from monopoly capitalism.

The victory of Italian fascism accelerated the ripening of fascist ideas in almost all the capitalist countries. But only the gravest economic crisis, which broke out on the background of the general post-war crisis of capitalism, brought about the victory of the second mass fascist organization set up in a highly developed capitalist country, namely, in Germany. I shall not dwell here on the differences between German and Italian fascism, or on the distinctions of their development. My aim here is to stress their similarities. German capitalism is more highly developed than Italian. But, defeated in the World War, deprived of its big army, navy, naval bases and colonies, German capitalism proved unable to compete with the great imperialist powers — just as Italian imperialism, too, despite its pretensions, was unable to compete because of the insufficiency of its raw material base, its inadequate capitalist accumulations and the lack of rich colonies. This inability to compete with England, the United States and France put German post-war monopoly capitalism in a worse position in the struggle against the growing danger of a proletarian revolution, which in 1918–1923 had been disrupted by German Social-Democracy. In the period of the temporary stabilization of capitalism, during which German capitalism regained a considerable part of its old positions on the world market, the German bourgeoisie was still able to retain its power, thanks to the assistance of Social-Democracy and to the fact that any attempt at revolutionary action on the part of the working class was suppressed. While making use of Social-Democracy as its main bulwark, the German bourgeoisie supported the fascist movement, partly as a means of bringing pressure to bear on Social-Democracy and of forcing it to decrease its demands, partly as a substitute for Social-Democracy in the future. The world economic crisis, which dealt the severest blows at Germany, confronted the German bourgeoisie with the problem of the imminent danger of a new revolution. No one could tell how long this crisis would continue. Its continuation carried with it the menace that the influence of German communism might grow to such an extent that the question of its winning over the majority of the working class — this main prerequisite of the struggle for the seizure of power — might become a question of the immediate future. Besides this, the crisis has let loose in all capitalist countries all centrifugal forces, tendencies to autarchy, *i.e.*, to carve out from the capitalist world the largest possible slice of territory as a closed field of exploitation for the monopolist bourgeoisie of the given nation. The German bourgeoisie had to take care to remove the danger of a proletarian revolution and, simultaneously, to create conditions for the utilization of the growing imperialist contradictions in order to create its own autarchic economic organism, *i.e.*, to conquer new colonies. These two problems could only be solved by destroying the remains of bourgeois democracy; without this, it was impossible either to defer or postpone the danger of a revolution, or to create the most favorable conditions for a new imperialist war. . . .

Summing up the phases of development of fascism in western Europe, it must be noted that its basic features are as follows: In the first place, fascism develops on the economic basis of the domination of monopoly capitalism, which is no longer able to solve the main economic problems facing society, which is feeling the approach of the social revolution and which is experiencing an everdeepening crisis. That means that reaction in countries of undeveloped capitalism, which have not yet reached the stage of monopoly capitalism, is not homogeneous with fascism, although it possesses many features in common with fascism (combination of savage terrorism with social demagogy). The absence of the domination of finance capital as an economic basis of fascism prevents those reactionary régimes from being the last phase of development on the way to socialism. They can still be swept away by bourgeois-democratic revolutions of a sufficiently prolonged character or even by some hybrid democratic régime, which may appear as the heir to a bankrupt reactionary régime, even without a revolution.

The second feature of fascism consists in the fact that it is not merely the bureaucratic rule of reactionary cliques, but a dictatorship resting upon mass organizations, mostly petty-bourgeois; that it combines the greatest terrorism against workers and revolutionary peasants with an unbridled social demagogy, which tries to cause disintegration among the working class, to draw over the most backward *lumpen*-proletarian sections of the working class into the camp of fascism. Fascism is not a mere restoration of bourgeois power. Such a restoration is an idle fancy, because in all countries of developed capitalism the old bourgeois power rested upon the support of the broad masses of the petty-bourgeoisie and even of the backward workers, who

supported all bourgeois and "Socialist" parties whose platform was the reform of capitalism. These masses were subordinated to the bourgeoisie through the medium of bourgeois democracy. Wherever bourgeois democracy has been done away with, it occurred precisely because the masses of the petty-bourgeoisie and of the proletariat have lost their faith in the stability of the capitalist system and have been leaving the ranks of the bourgeois parties in greater numbers every day.

Fascist dictatorship is not simply a reactionary dictatorship, like the régime of Horthy or Tsankov.[2] It is a dictatorship of finance capital, which has been able, by employing a number of new methods, to secure for itself the support of the petty bourgeoisie by means of a demagogic policy and mass organizations.

Do these two features of fascism — (1) the domination of a monopoly capitalism, which has already been shaken, which fears a proletarian revolution, which is seeking an escape from it by way of a fascist state organization within the country, and a new war with the object of a redivision of the world, and (2) a striving to create, as a bulwark for capitalism, a mass petty-bourgeois movement, hoodwinked by Social-Democratic slogans — exist in Japan? Undoubtedly these two features do exist. Finance capital rules in Japan. Students who stress the peculiar traits of the rule of finance capital in Japan — the fact that it still rules to a large extent through the monopoly of banks, through the exploitation of the small and middle *entrepreneurs* and the scattered small farmers by the banks, the fact that it has merged to a great extent with the survivals of feudalism — such students are absolutely right. . . . The importance of these factors lies, first, in the fact that insufficient concentration and inadequate technical modernization of Japanese industry do not allow Japanese

[2] In Hungary and Bulgaria. [Editor's note]

finance capital to develop that strength without which Japanese imperialism, to employ the correct expression of one of our students of Japanese affairs, may prove a "powerful fist upon very feeble muscles." The Japanese militarists are well aware of this weakness and during the last two years they have done all in their power to concentrate industry and equip it with modern technique. Nevertheless, despite the large sums invested in industry during the last two years by the Japanese government and Japanese financial trusts, they have not succeeded in removing this backwardness to any considerable extent. The exceptional parasitism of the Japanese landlord, who squeezes out of the countryside 50 per cent of its annual income, and the presence of survivals of feudalism in all spheres of rural life, are a pledge that the future will bring with it a broad upswing of the democratic revolutionary movement among the peasantry. However, important as these peculiarities are, we cannot evade that question which is indeed the crux of all questions. And in considering Japanese imperialism and Japanese fascism, the question is: Who is economic master in Japan — monopoly capitalism or the survivals of feudalism? To this question there can be only one answer.

The development of Japan since 1868 denotes the rise and triumph of industrial capitalism, its transition to monopoly capitalism. The landowner class of Japan — a survival of the feudal class which was not swept away in 1868 — has managed to retain, though in a modified form, its right to collect tribute from the peasantry. To this end they have used the state power, which they have retained to a considerable extent in their own hands. But this power has at the same time served as a means of strengthening finance capital, has served to assist its victory over all other classes in Japan, has served as a weapon in its struggle for the world market and for winning positions on the Asiatic continent. The landowner class, which invests in industry and the banks the capital which it squeezes out of the peasantry, is itself a part of the monopolist bourgeoisie. Inasmuch as its interests as a rent collector have conflicted with its interests as a profit owner, it could get its own specific interests served at the expense of the general development of the economic forces of the country. But the landowner class of Japan, thus strengthening the rôle of monopoly capital as a brake on the development of the productive forces, could not rule in contradiction to the basic interests of monopoly capitalism. From the capitalist development of Japan the landowner tried to snatch for himself as much as possible, but he could not pursue a policy which did not conform to the basic interests of monopoly capitalism.

The entire economic and political crisis of Japan is unfolding against a background formed by the crisis of monopoly capitalism, although this crisis is deepened and complicated by the presence of survivals of feudalism. The social and political crisis of Japan has the same causes as the crisis of the entire capitalist system. Monopoly capitalism has lost the ability to secure the development of the productive forces. Every one of its attempts to do this by way of improved technique or rationalization leads to a tremendous intensification of the distress and unemployment of the masses, enhances the social crisis. The attempt of Japanese monopoly capitalism to conquer new markets for the sale of its products leads to the tremendous sharpening of international imperialist antagonisms, compels it to arm at frantic speed. These armaments, undermining as they do the economic forces of the countryside, impose an unheard-of burden on the masses of the working class and of the urban and petty bourgeoisie, and, in their turn, weaken the productive forces of the country. The attempt to conquer parts of China, in order to create an autarchic Japanese colonial empire on the continent, having its own iron and coal and forming a market closed to other imperialist powers, leads to increasing conflict with the masses, who do not want to become the colonial slaves of Japan, and to a conflict with other imperialist powers, above all with the United States.

Such are the bases of the crisis which Japan is experiencing. It is only a modification of the general crisis which is being experienced by monopoly capitalism. Under the circumstances, the danger of a proletarian revolution in Japan is beyond doubt and arises from fundamentally the same sources as in other countries — from the domination of monopoly capitalism. Survivals of feudalism in Japan, sharpening as they do the antagonisms of interests between the peasantry and the landlord class, create the danger of revolutionary peasant movements and thus create conditions for the support of a proletarian revolution by a peasant war. . . .

. . . The fact that survivals of feudalism exist in Japan, and that consequently there is a prospect of a proletarian revolution in Japan growing out of the bourgeois-democratic revolution, does not do away with the fact that the degree of development reached by Japanese capitalism is one of monopoly capitalism. The outcome of the crisis of monopoly capitalism can only be a social revolution, no matter through how many stages it will have to pass. The crisis in Japan is developing on the basis of monopoly capitalism, and the Japanese bourgeoisie, seeking a way out of the crisis by way of imperialist aggression and fascism, is seeking salvation from a proletarian revolution and is struggling for such terms of competition with other imperialist powers as may enable her to avoid a proletarian revolution in the future as well. There is, therefore, not the slightest doubt that Japanese fascism is in the main trying to solve those very problems which German and

Italian fascism are also trying to solve. When the authors of this book write that:

West European fascism is in the main a tool of finance capital, while the Japanese reactionary chauvinist movement, taken as a whole, is a tool not of finance capital alone, but also of Japanese monarchy, which represents a *bloc* of two class forces — finance capital and semi-feudal landlords,

they are mistaken both with regard to western European and with regard to Japanese fascism in that they contrast the landlords to finance capitalism.

The Italian landowners, trying to escape the onslaught of the farm laborers and small tenants, played a great rôle in the victory of Italian fascism. The rôle of the German *Junkers* in the victory of German fascism is known to the whole world. Detachments of fascist murderers were reared on the Mecklenburg, Pomeranian and East-Elbian estates, long before gold from the iron safes of captains of industry began to pour into the pockets of fascism. A good many of the leaders of German fascism are sons of landowners. German fascism came to power easily thanks to the support given it by the Prussian *Junkers*, Field-Marshal Hindenburg, and the officers of the *Reichswehr*, who consisted of Prussian *Junkers*. That is why German fascism does not dare to infringe upon the interests of the East-Elbian landowners, notwithstanding the fact that it has to play the rôle of a party whose alleged aim is to save the peasantry. Owing to the fact that the survivals of feudalism in Japan are stronger than in Italy and even in Germany, the rôle of the landlords in the military-fascist movement of Japan is surely more powerful. But, in the main, it cannot differ from the rôle of the landowners in the European fascist movement, because fascism in Japan, by its armaments policy, is above all filling the pockets of finance capital. Having seized power completely, the policy which it pursued in the economic sphere could only be one which in the main suited the interests of monopoly capital. By their participation in the fascist movement, the landowners have secured for themselves a special portion of the general imperialist loot, just as the German and Italian landowners did. It is possible that their share in the partition of the temporary plunder will be even larger. But that does not mean that any of the bases of Japanese fascism are fundamentally different from the fascism of western Europe.

The second feature of the fascist movement, namely the search for a bulwark among the broad petty-bourgeois masses, who are attracted by a broad demagogic social program, is to be observed in Japan no less than in Europe.

This very book offers thousands of proofs that there is not one social idea, promulgated for demagogic purposes by European fascism, which is not to be found in the arsenal of the fascist movement in Japan. Could there be a better example of social demagogy than when Japanese noblemen spoke at the trial of Inukai's murderers as defenders of workers and peasants? It is precisely thanks to this social demagogy, that Japanese military-fascist organizations have succeeded in mobilizing huge masses of the petty bourgeoisie who have been set in motion by the social and political crisis in Japan. The authors of this book are right when they prove that the figures produced by Japanese fascists to show the strength of their organization are greatly exaggerated. But it would also be a mistake to underrate these forces. The point is not whether the Japanese fascists have millions of adherents, united into special fascist party organizations, or whether these millions are in mass organizations of a general patriotic nature, created by the bureaucrats and militarists. The decisive question is whether those people who control these mass organizations, although officially non-fascist, serve fascism or not, and what kind

of ideas they propound in these organizations. . . . The distrust felt by the bureaucratic military leaders of Japan for an organization of the petty-bourgeois masses, their fear of this organization, is driving the military clique towards an attempt to seize power without any organization of a fascist mass party, just as in Germany this same fear of the petty-bourgeois masses led to the formation of the government of von Papen and Schleicher, who tried to retain power without Hitler, and, to some extent, against him. But that government was no more than an episode, for, without the support of mass fascist organizations, it was left hanging in the air. The course of development in Japan is difficult to foretell, but if the Araki group seizes complete power by way of backstairs machinations, backed by the pressure of the upper strata of the officers, then this group will have to look for support to the fascist organizations. Whether it is a government basing itself on fascist organizations, or whether it develops into a government of the fascist organizations — its social composition will be the same: it will be a dictatorship of monopoly capitalism, forced to give great consideration to the interest of the landowners; and in either case the petty bourgeoisie will not govern, but serve only as a mass bulwark for the domination of monopoly capitalism.

The peculiarities of Japanese fascism consist to a certain extent in the more considerable part played by the landlords in the organization of Japanese fascism in the spirit of the Middles Ages, or, to speak more exactly, of those legends about the Middle Ages with which the leaders of Japanese fascism are trying to imbue the masses of the people. Here, however, we are dealing with secondary, not with primary differences. The most important, though still not the main, difference is the rôle of the Japanese army as organizer and leader of the fascist movement. In

Italy the army officers did not play this rôle, although a number of the higher commanders sided with fascism. The Italian army did not come out of the World War crowned with glory, while the masses of the Italian people were utterly war-weary. It was therefore only after its victory that Italian fascism got the army under its control. In Germany it was only the younger generation of the former imperial army — those who had not entered the *Reichswehr* — who played a leading rôle in the fascist movement. The *Reichswehr* secretly rendered aid to the fascist organizations, supplying them with arms and instructors. However, from military-political considerations and partly owing to its connection with the old bourgeois parties and their régime, it was unable to play a leading rôle in the rise and victory of German fascism. In Japan, however, we see the higher officers playing this leading rôle in the organization of fascist forces. . . . This rôle of the Japanese officers in the organization of fascism is to be explained, on the one hand, by the halo which surrounds them as the organizers of the victorious war against Russia in 1904–05, and on the other hand, by the fact that the ruin of a considerable part of the small and middle landowners, from whom the most of the officers are recruited, and the degradation of Japanese agriculture are creating social unrest among the officers, allying them with the discontented petty-bourgeoisie, from whom a part of the officers also comes. The rôle of the Japanese officers as leaders of the fascist movement has created among the higher circles of these officers, rallied around General Araki, the illusion that this group can seize power alone, without the participation of fascist petty-bourgeois organizations, which the Araki group does not try to unite apparently from fear of giving them too much importance. But this policy arouses discontent among a section of the junior officers, headed by . . .

Colonel Hashimoto, who declares that the officers are not able to rule Japan and that unless they create a mass fascist party as their bulwark, they will be routed by communism which is undoubtedly developing into a mass organized power. The purely fascist tendency represented by Hashimoto, which will increase in strength with the growth of the social crisis in Japan, shows that here too there are forces which (as far as the rôle of the army in the fascist movement is concerned) bring Japanese fascism close to the European type.

The mistakes committed by the authors of this work flow from two sources. One of these is that from a legitimate fear of underrating the importance of survivals of feudalism they have in their final formulations been guilty to a certain extent of going to the other extreme. The other is that the historical exposition of the development of the Japanese fascist movement leaves an excessively marked imprint on their theoretical deductions. The fascist movement in Japan has its roots in the bureaucratic-military organization of the Black Dragon, which in the past was the main secret organization of budding Japanese imperialism. But despite its landowner-bureaucratic composition this organization, serving as it did the aims of Japanese expansionism, was in the last analysis a tool of monopoly capitalism. . . . Marxist analysis cannot of course disregard the social composition of any political organization, but it does not admit that this social composition is the decisive factor in determining the social character of a given movement; it asks what class interests in the last analysis are directing this movement. The parties of the Second International in all capitalist countries are in the majority of cases still workers' parties in their composition, but they are bourgeois parties in the character of their policy, because, renouncing the revolutionary struggle, they cannot pursue any other policy than that dictated by the interests of the bourgeoisie. The fascist parties in western Europe are, in their composition, petty-bourgeois parties. Their leading strata are to a large extent landowners, but they pursue a policy of defending the interests of finance capital, which represents the leading force of a capitalist society which has reached the stage of monopoly capitalism. And the same holds true of Japan, although the leading rôle in the fascist movement of that country is played by the landowners and the higher bureaucracy.

Characteristics of Japanese "Fascism"

MARUYAMA MASAO

Among Japanese scholars Professor Maruyama has provided some of the most incisive and original analyses of the development of nationalism in Japan since the Tokugawa period. The following passages from his essays are relevant to the question whether pre-war Japan can be regarded as a fascist state and, if so, whether Japanese fascism differed fundamentally from the European varieties.

THE Japanese "fascist" [1] movement naturally had elements in common with the fascist ideology current in the world. It shared the ideology of its Italian and German counterparts in such matters as the rejection of the world view of individualistic liberalism, opposition to parliamentary politics which is the political expression of liberalism, insistence on foreign expansion, a tendency to glorify military build-up and war, a strong emphasis on racial myths and the national essence, a rejection of class warfare based on totalitarianism, and the struggle against Marxism. Again, there is a great similarity between Eastern and Western "fascism" in the way of thinking that lies at the root of these concrete demands. For example, Ōkawa Shūmei provides the following estimate of capitalism and socialism:

The struggle between capitalism and socialism is not one of principle. Both stand on the same principle, and the struggle concerns simply its practical realization. . . . On the one hand, pure capitalism attempts to limit the possession of material wealth to a smaller number of people, that is, to the small number

of people called the capitalist class. On the other hand, socialism attempts to distribute material wealth among a large number of workers. Both are attempts to cause this cherished material wealth to be owned on the one hand by a small circle, on the other by a large circle. Both agree in setting an extreme value on material matters, in finding the true happiness of mankind in material pleasures and hence in considering the object of mankind to lie in the abundant possession of material things.[2]

Ōkawa goes on to say

If the way of thought that places material things above the human personality is not reformed, nothing good can be expected from attempts to overthrow the capitalist economic system and to transform it into a socialist system.[3]

This is the essence of his criticism: since both capitalism and socialism stand on the same materialist basis, socialism is incapable of providing any real relief for the defects of modern civilization; both socialism and Marxism are beasts from the same den

[1] The quotation marks around "fascist" have been added by the editor of this volume.

[2] "The Way of Japan and the Japanese" (*Nihon oyobi Nihonjin no Michi*).
[3] "The Way of Japan and the Japanese" (*Nihon oyobi Nihonjin no Michi*).

From Maruyama Masao *Thought and Behaviour in Modern Japanese Politics*, Ivan Morris, ed., pp. 34–6, 52–7, 76–8 (London: Oxford University Press, 1963).

as capitalism. This closely resembles the ideology of Nazi and Italian "fascism," which says the same thing in different words.

The stress on "idealism" and "spirituality" as against materialism in the "fascist" ideology signifies in reality an attempt to divert the eyes of the people from the fundamental contradictions of the social structure; in place of real structural reforms, they aim at reforms within the minds of men, that is, reforms in the way of thinking. This provides the real explanation of why "fascism" eventually performed the role of serving monopolistic capital, despite its having displayed a certain anti-capitalist appearance at the outset. None of these points can be called distinctive characteristics of Japanese "fascism."

*   *   *

What mainly characterizes the formation of the Japanese radical "fascist" movement from the Blood Pledge Corps Incident until the February Incident is that until the very last its practical managers had no mass organization and showed no particular zeal for organizing the masses. Rather they made it from first to last a movement of a limited number of "patriots." The heroism, or the consciousness of the "patriot" bound up with the Japanese movement acted as a check on its development on a mass basis. For example, Tachibana Kōsaburō in his "Principles of the Japanese Patriotic Reformation" writes as follows:

What I now emphasize, and ask you all to engrave on your hearts, is the cardinal fact that a nation-wide social reformation can be initiated only by a group of patriots who are capable of pursuing the great aim of saving the country and relieving the people in accordance with the will of Heaven. . . . Needless to say, the number of patriots who can be found to initiate this great task at the sacrifice of their lives will never be large. But it is also a fact that scattered among

all classes of society there are patriots who can carry out the will of Heaven if it chooses them to do so . . . People who call for reformation must be willing to sacrifice their lives for the people. Only a group of patriots who would sacrifice their lives for the great aim of saving the country and relieving the people can be the leaders of a national reform movement. In view of the present state of Japan, such patriots can be found only among you military men, and it is above all the farmers who will respond to your call. This is why I must ask you to contemplate deeply and to make an iron decision.

In this way Tachibana whipped up the strong patriotic spirit of the military class, which was already imbued with what Nietzsche called "the pathos of distance."

Because of this basic idea, the movement naturally developed as a visionary idealism of a minority and failed to organize and mobilize the masses. This was allied to other distinctive characteristics, such as its extreme fantasy, abstraction and lack of plan. The radical movement was always governed by the mythological optimism that, if patriots led the way by destructive action, a future course would become clear. For instance, the thought of Inoue Nisshō, the leader of the Blood Pledge Corps Incident, is described in the court judgment as follows:

To overthrow the old system of organization is a destructive or negative act. To establish the new system of organization is a constructive or positive act. Without destruction, however, there can be no construction. Since ultimate denial is the same as genuine affirmation, destruction is itself construction, and the two are one and inseparable.

During the trial Inoue himself stated, "it is more correct to say that I have no systematized ideas. I transcend reason and act completely upon intuition." He deliberately rejected any theory for constructive planning after the rising.

Again, the May 15 Incident was the first

relatively organized act of violence of radical "fascism," and fairly detailed plans were prepared for the uprising. Let us take, for example, the plan for the first stage by the Navy group. One section was to attack the Premier's residence and Count Makino, and promulgate martial law with the support of Admiral Tōgō. A second section was to attack the Industrialists' Club and the Peers' Assembly Hall, enter the Premier's residence and begin the task of national reconstruction with the support of Gondō Seikyō. A third section was to attack the headquarters of the Minsei Tō and the Seiyū Kai, and following that to release the Blood Pledge Corps men from prison. Thus a fairly detailed program was drawn up; yet it is not at all clear what concrete reforms were to be made, other than that Gondō was to be the brains of the new government. On this point Lieutenant Koga declared in court:

We thought about destruction first. We never considered taking on the duty of construction. We foresaw, however, that once the destruction was accomplished, someone would take charge of the construction for us. We had no guiding principle, but thought to set up a military government after first proclaiming martial law. . . . When I called on Major-General Araki in Kumamoto in December 1930 with the late Major Fujii, he told us that the deadlock in the national situation must be broken by the Yamato spirit. At that time I trusted and respected Major-General Araki. In 1932 key positions in the Army such as Director of Military Police and of Civilian Defense were filled by men of Araki's following. We believed that, if we could create a situation requiring martial law, a military government would be set up round Araki as War Minister, and a start made upon the path of reconstruction.[4]

Thus, because of the idea that "We should just destroy; afterwards something will emerge, and someone else take over the construction," the plan went no further than setting up a military government.

Here, however, there is a difference of views between the Army and the Navy defendants. The Army group had not thought even as far ahead as setting up a military government under martial law. For example, an Army cadet, Ishizeki Sakae, stated, "It is said that the Navy group had thought in advance of the martial law edict, but we wished to die fighting and did not think of the results beforehand." Here the lack of realism is much more extreme.

This same characteristic may be seen in the Heaven-Sent Soldiers' Unit Incident. . . . It ended abortively, but in the original plan, 3,600 men were to be mobilized at 11 A.M. on July 7, 1933. First, the person responsible for the air attack was to drop bombs on the Premier's residence, the residence of the Privy Seal, Count Makino, and the Metropolitan Police Headquarters. Leaflets were also to be distributed, and the plane was to land in front of the Imperial Palace in exact timing with an attack on the Metropolitan Police Headquarters by the ground forces. The ground forces were then to divide into several sections. One section armed with pistols and swords was to attack the Premier's residence and kill any surviving Cabinet Ministers. Other sections were to attack the residences of Count Makino and of the Presidents of the Seiyū Kai and the Minsei Tō as well as the Japan Industrialists' Club and the Headquarters of the Socialist Masses Party. Another section was to break into armouries and seize arms and ammunition. After the attack on the Metropolitan Police Headquarters the main section was to occupy the Industrial Bank of Japan. From this stronghold they were to fight to the death against the police units of the entire city, while exerting themselves in propaganda activities. Much thought went into this plan, but it ends in death in battle. It is striking that the planning did not go beyond battle strategy.

[4] Tōkyō Asahi, evening edition, July 29, 1933.

Finally we come to the February Incident. This was the radical "fascist" movement in its largest production, with a well-planned and organized character rarely seen in Japanese uprisings. According to the prosecution indictments and the judgment reports, this rising was aimed at realizing Kita Ikki's "General Outline of Measures for the Reconstruction of Japan." But the accused officers unanimously denied this. For instance, [one of them] states:

By "Restoration" we meant our desire to uphold a spiritual reformation of the people and to make material reconstruction subsequent to it. . . . How could we fellow patriots have been able to carry out this scheme if we had nourished political ambitions or indulged in private fancies about the actual structure of the government?

In response to the question, "Is not destruction without construction pure recklessness?" he replied,

What is destruction? What is construction? . . . To destroy the wicked is to reveal the path of righteousness. Destroying the wicked and revealing the path of righteousness are one and inseparable, like back and front. The punishment of evil men and restoration are the same thing.

He concludes with the same "logic" as Inoue's: "Once the great moral cause is clarified, and the hearts of the people rectified, the Imperial Way cannot fail to be promoted." . . .

Thus the pattern of the radical "fascist" movement was almost invariably characterized by fantasy and lack of realism. This is best revealed by the fact that mobilization of one thousand six hundred troops in the February Incident resulted in nothing more than the murder of a few elderly men.

This point also marks a clear difference between "fascism" in Japan and Germany. As a result of the strong survival in its ideology of a mediaeval [type of] patriotism, . . . this sort of patriotism came to appear in the concrete "fascist" movement as well. Democracy was flatly rejected by Japanese "fascism," but not by the Nazis.[5] The Nazis decried Weimar democracy, but not democracy in general. Rather the aim of the Nazis was to stigmatize Weimar and Anglo-American democracy as a Jewish plutocracy and to proclaim themselves a "true" Nordic democracy. Of course this claim was simply "the democratic disguise for dictatorship," to borrow the words of Professor Miyazawa. However, the fact that it was constrained to appear in a democratic disguise reveals that even in Germany democracy had already struck ineradicable roots in the political ideology of the nation.

Hitler was strongly opposed to the monarchism of some Junkers, and was himself fundamentally a republican. In *Mein Kampf* he sharply distinguishes monarchic patriotism from the patriotism that loves the fatherland and the people, and he ridicules the tendency to worship State power for its own sake as animalian worship. He maintained that "States exist for men, and not men for States." Such a way of thinking is accepted as a matter of course only after the experience of a bourgeois democratic revolution. This naturally gave the Nazi movement a clear mass character from the outset. Again, it is stated in *Mein Kampf* that "The previous Pan-Germanism was splendid as an ideology but failed be-

---

[5] But note what Kita Ikki has to say on the subject: ". . . as the commanding figure in the national movement and as complete representative of the modern democratic country, [the Emperor] has become representative of the nation. In other words, since the Meiji Revolution, Japan has become a modern democratic state with the emperor as political nucleus. Is there any need whatever for us to import a direct translation of the "democracy" of others as though we lacked something? . . . Do not jump to the conclusion that this is a shortcoming we are seeking to correct. We have already advanced farther than some other countries as a democratic country." (Kita Ikki, *Nihon Kaizō Hōan*, loc. cit.) [Editor's note]

cause it did not possess a mass organization."

But the Japanese "fascist" movement from below remained to the last a movement of a small number of patriots — visionary, fanatic and lacking in plan. These are the striking tendencies in the formation of the Japanese "fascist" movement. Of course mythological elements and the idea of an elite are common to all fascist ideologies. The differences in the degree to which these were held in Japan, however, are so marked as to amount to qualitative differences.

*   *   *

Why in Japan did "fascism" from below, the "fascist" movement that arose among civilians, fail to grasp hegemony? This is a crucial question, and any answer must emphasize the following point. In the process of "fascization" the strength of influences from the lower stratum of society is prescribed by, among other things, the extent to which a democratic movement has taken place in the country concerned. In Italy before the March on Rome the Socialist Party was the leading party in the Assembly. In the case of Germany we note again the powerful influence of the Social Democratic and Communist Parties just before the Nazi revolution. Both the Nazis and the Fascists could draw in the masses only by flaunting themselves as the exponents of true socialism and as the party of the workers. This bespeaks the power of the mass movement in Germany and even in Italy, and is the reason that popular bases had to be preserved to some extent in the "fascist" organization if only for deception.

How does this compare with the situation in our country? Of course in Japan too the labour movement had made an unprecedented advance from about 1926, and because of the crisis in rural tenancy disputes had increased rapidly year by year. As we have seen, the Japanese "fascist" movement flourished in the background of these conditions and appeared on the scene as a reaction to the left-wing movement. In this respect it can be said to follow the rules. But today it is quite clear to any observer that the left-wing movement did not in fact permeate to the workers and farmers to a degree comparable with that in Germany and Italy. It would be going too far to suggest that the overwhelming influence of Marxism was a phenomenon confined to the educated class — to the lecture platforms and journals that this class supported; its power was felt in many other areas also. Yet it is doubtful whether the menace of bolshevism in Japan was even as real as the ruling class and the conservative circles proclaimed.

The progress of Japanese "fascist" transformation was very gradual. There was no March on Rome and no January 30, 1933; this suggests the weakness of resistance from below. There were no organized labour or proletarian parties to be smashed. Here we should note the form of Japanese monopoly capital itself. When we consider the population structure in 1930, directly before the Manchurian Incident when the Japanese "fascist" movement suddenly became vigorous, we find that the number of labourers employed in workshops of five or more people was 2,032,000, and the number of casual workers 1,963,000. In contrast, employees in commerce numbered 2,200,-000, government officials and company employees 1,800,000 and small traders 1,500,-000. One understands how small in numbers the true proletariat was compared with the medium and small businessmen and the salaried class. As another example, in the League of Nations Statistical Yearbook for 1926, Japan's industrial population (including domestic industries) is given as 19.4% of the total population. When this is compared with, for example, Britain

(39.7%), France (33.9%), Belgium (39.5%), Holland (36.1%) and Germany (35.8%), it becomes clear how inferior the industrialization of Imperial Japan was compared with that of the European capitalist nations.

At the peak of the Japanese social structure stood monopoly capital, rationalized to the highest degree. But at its base were crammed together minute-scale agriculture with production methods that had scarcely changed since feudal times and household industries almost entirely dependent on the labour of members of the family. The most advanced and the most primitive techniques exist side by side in a stratified industrial structure. Production forms of different historical stages overlie and supplement each other. This was a decisive obstacle to the growth of an organized democratic movement in Japanese politics. On the one hand there is the stubborn rule of absolutism, on the other the development of monopoly capital, both in agreement and reinforcing each other.

This may also have determined the fate of the Japanese "fascist" movement as we have observed it above. Here is revealed the internal weakness of the "fascism" from below in Japan.

Differences between Nazi and Japanese Leaders

MARUYAMA MASAO

Professor Maruyama has also made some penetrating comparisons between the German Nazi leaders and their opposite numbers in Japan. This selection is taken from his "Thought and Behaviour of Japan's Wartime Leaders."

ONE does not have to be an adherent of Freud to recognize that "fascism" is invariably linked with an abnormal psychological condition and to a greater or lesser extent accompanied by symptoms of hysteria. In this respect there is no particular difference between its Western and Eastern varieties. There is, however, a quite remarkable gap between the actual forms in which this abnormal psychology expressed itself in Nazi Germany and in wartime Japan.

First and foremost, the background of the Nazi leaders differed diametrically from that of our own war criminals. Most of the top Nazis had enjoyed very little formal education and, until they actually seized power, few of them had held any position worthy of the name.[1]

[1] Göbbels (with his title of D.Phil. from Heidelberg) was an exception that proved the rule. Most of the others, far from being ashamed of their humble origins, regarded their lack of social status and education as a cause for pride, and used it successfully to suggest how close they were to the masses. Directly after seizing power Hitler addressed the workers in a Berlin factory as follows:

> Deutsche Volksgenossen und Volksgenossinnen! Meine deutschen Arbeiter! If I speak today to you and to millions of other workers, I do so with greater right than any other. I have myself come from your ranks. I have been among you for four and a half years in war, and I speak now to you to whom I belong . . . I

The prisoners in the dock at Tokyo, however, were all "men of talent": they had attended the foremost educational or the military colleges, and after graduation had travelled along the smooth highway of advancement until they came to occupy the highest official positions in the Empire.

There was also a significant difference in personality. The Nazi leaders were a collection of freaks, including drug addicts, sexual perverts and alcoholics.[2] By and large they were beyond the pale of normal society; they were, in fact, essentially "outlaws."

Among our defendants too there were some genuine psychopaths . . . and others . . . who were borderline cases. Yet, however obscure and irrational their political judgment and behaviour may have been, as a group they can hardly be considered to have been mentally abnormal by nature. Far from being excluded from normal society, they usually enjoyed the most enviable positions, either basking in the re-

lead the struggle for the million-masses of our brave, industrious workers and our labouring people . . . I need no title. My name, which I earned by my own strength, is my title. (Frederick Schuman: "The Nazi Dictatorship", p. 259.)

Even if Tōjō had wanted to make such a speech, he could never have done it.

[2] e.g. Göring, Himmler, Ley.

From Maruyama Masao, *Thought and Behaviour in Modern Japanese Politics*, Ivan Morris, ed., pp. 90–5 (London: Oxford University Press, 1963).

flected glory of impressive ancestors or having been cut out since their youth to become ministers or generals. As regards personality, none of them was a pure outlaw.

To be sure, some members of the military clique, especially certain Army officers, were not entirely lacking in the "outlaw" aspect; but even they were guided in equal measure by a timid, bureaucratic mentality, which became more and more pronounced as they rose in the hierarchy.

The true outlaw type did play an important part in Japanese "fascism." But, as the name *rōnin* suggests, one of their characteristics was precisely that they did *not* attain any influential position; instead these eerie gentry operated behind the scenes, scurrying in and out of the offices of the men in power, and receiving an unfixed income in return for such services as they could render. This Japanese type of outlaw differed entirely from his Nazi counterpart.

The Class A war crime suspects in Japan, far from being the prime movers, can rather be regarded as pathetic robots, manipulated by outlaws (some big and some small; some belonging to the government and some outside) on whom they looked down from the height of their positions. Here we are confronted with a most important contrast between the Western and Eastern manifestations of "fascism," a contrast noticed by the Prosecuting Attorney, Mr. Tavenner, when he wound up his closing address to the Court as follows:

These men were not the hoodlums who were the powerful part of the group which stood before the tribunal at Nuremberg, dregs of a criminal environment thoroughly schooled in the ways of crime, and knowing no other methods but those of crime. These men were supposed to be the elite of the nation, the honest and trusted leaders to whom the fate of the nation had been confidently entrusted. . . . These men knew the difference between good and evil. . . . With full knowledge they voluntarily made their choice for evil. . . . With full knowledge they voluntarily elected to follow the path of war bringing death and injury to millions of human beings and hate wherever their forces went . . . For this choice they must bear the guilt.

It is clear, then, that the defendants in Tōkyō cannot themselves be regarded as mentally abnormal. Their thought and behaviour are relevant to the psychopathology of fascism only to the extent that they were infected by people, in Japan and abroad, who were abnormal. There is no doubt that they were infected by the upsurge of Nazism in Europe. The operative factor, however, was not Nazism itself but the foundation that it provided.

Scholars have already examined the socio-economic basis of the differences between the two countries. My approach to the problem will be a more direct one, namely, to compare the words and actions of the wartime leaders in Germany and Japan.

German and Japanese "fascism" left the same trail of destruction, chaos and destitution in the world; but there is a striking contrast between the situation in Germany, where thought and behaviour were entirely consistent, and that in Japan, where the two were remarkably at variance. On August 22, 1939, the day before Hitler's decision to invade Poland, he addressed his generals as follows:

I shall give a propagandist reason for starting the war — never mind whether it is plausible or not. The victor will not be asked afterward whether he told the truth or not. In starting and waging a war it is not right that matters, but victory.

What an inexorable conclusion, and how uncannily it reveals what Karl Levitt refers to as "active nihilism"!

No class of militarist in our country ever dared voice so categorical a view. Much as they believed in private that "he who wins is always in the right," they lacked the courage to state this openly as the guiding principle of their decisions. Instead they always tried to find some way to conceal or moralize it. Thus the suppression of foreign peoples by Japanese military might was always "the promulgation of the Imperial Way" and was regarded as an act of benevolence towards the foreigners in question. The attitude was unconsciously caricatured in a speech by General Araki in 1933:

Needless to say, the Imperial Army's spirit lies in exalting the Imperial Way and spreading the National Virtue. Every single bullet must be charged with the Imperial Way and the end of every bayonet must have the National Virtue burnt into it. If there are any who oppose the Imperial Way or the National Virtue, we shall give them an injection with this bullet and this bayonet.

Men who could think like this would not be satisfied until they had imbued each individual slaughter with the mystique of the Imperial Way.

Now let us hear what a German leader has to say about the treatment of subject peoples: "What happens to a Russian, to a Czech, does not interest me in the slightest," declared Heinrich Himmler on October 4, 1943.

Whether nations live in prosperity or starve to death like cattle [continued Himmler] interests me only in so far as we need them as slaves to our *Kultur;* otherwise it is of no interest to me.

Whether ten thousand Russian females fall down from exhaustion while digging an antitank ditch interests me only in so far as the antitank ditch for Germany is finished. . . .

The S.S. leader's lucidity is nothing short of breathtaking!

The Nazis were of course second to none when it came to disseminating sweetsounding slogans in Germany and abroad.

They seem to have been perfectly aware, however, of what was true in their slogans and what was mere propaganda. Our own wartime leaders, on the contrary, were ultimately taken in by the slogans that they themselves had concocted, and as a result their view of reality was hopelessly obfuscated. The cross-examination of General Minami Jirō, the former Governor-General of Korea, provides a good example:

President of the Court: Why did you call it a "Holy War"?
Minani: I used the word because it was in wide currency at the time.
Q: What was holy about it?
A: I never thought about that very deeply. I used the word because it was in wide currency at that time among the general public. My idea was that this was not an aggressive war but one that had arisen owing to unavoidable circumstances.

The same tendency to be taken in by one's own moralizing slogans can be seen in the case of General Matsui Iwane, the former Commander-in-Chief of the Japanese expeditionary force in Shanghai. In his deposition he defined the true nature of the China Incident as follows:

The struggle between Japan and China was always a fight between brothers within the "Asian family" . . . It has been my belief during all these years that we must regard this struggle as a method of making the Chinese undergo self-reflection. We do not do this because we hate them, but on the contrary because we love them too much. It is just the same in a family when an elder brother has taken all that he can stand from his illbehaved younger brother and has to chastise him in order to make him behave properly.

One might imagine that this argument was trumped up for the benefit of the trial, but in fact it appears that the general really believed his talk about brotherly love. For already in 1937, when he was about to leave for Shanghai he told the supporters of the Greater Asia Association at a farewell party: "I am going to the front not to fight an enemy but in the state of mind of one who sets out to pacify his brother."

The type of psychology according to which one chastises people because one loves them too much led to atrocities like the "rape of Nanking," before which we must cover our eyes in shame. What our wartime leaders accomplished by their moralizing was not simply to deceive the people of Japan or of the world; more than anyone else they deceived themselves.

III. JAPANISM

JAPANESE ULTRA-NATIONALISM AND ITS CON-
COMITANTS BELONG TO A DIFFERENT CATEGORY
FROM FASCISM OR MILITARISM IN THE WEST,
AND CAN BE UNDERSTOOD ONLY IN TERMS OF
CERTAIN UNIQUE ASPECTS OF JAPAN'S IDEOLOG-
ICAL, RELIGIOUS, SOCIAL, AND INTERNATIONAL
DEVELOPMENT.

The Unique National Polity (Kokutai no Hongi)

JAPAN MINISTRY OF EDUCATION

Of the many works aimed at explaining the uniqueness of Japan's "national polity" none was more influential than "The Principles of National
Polity" (*Kokutai no Hongi*). Published by the Ministry of Education in 1937,
it sold more than two million copies and gave official sanction to many theories about "Japanism" that until then had been propagated largely by independent nationalist extremists. To what extent (if any) is the approach sug-
gested by the following selection compatible with fascism? Is Bushido, as these
writers expound it, essentially different from what we normally understand
by militarism?

INTRODUCTION: PRESENT-DAY JAPAN
AND HER IDEOLOGIES

The various ideological and social evils
of present-day Japan are the result of ignoring the fundamental and running after the
trivial, of lack of judgment, and a failure
to digest things thoroughly; and this is due
to the fact that since the days of Meiji so
many aspects of European and American
culture, systems, and learning, have been
imported, and that, too rapidly. As a matter of fact, the foreign ideologies imported
into our country are in the main ideologies
of the Enlightenment that have come down
from the eighteenth century, or extensions
of them. The views of the world and of life
that form the basis of these ideologies are
a rationalism and a positivism, lacking in
historical views, which on the one hand lay
the highest value on, and assert the liberty

From *Kokutai no Hongi — Cardinal Principles of the National Entity of Japan*, tr. by J. O. Gaunt-
lett, ed. by R. K. Hall (Cambridge, Mass.: Harvard University Press). [The editor has mostly followed the adaptation given in *Sources of the Japanese Tradition*, pp. 786–94.]

and equality of, individuals, and on the other hand lay value on a world by nature abstract, transcending nations and races. Consequently, importance is laid upon human beings and their groupings, who have become isolated from historical entireties, abstract and independent of each other. It is political, social, moral, and pedagogical theories based on such views of the world and of life, that have on the one hand made contributions to the various reforms seen in our country, and on the other have had deep and wide influence on our nation's primary ideology and culture. . . .

CONSCIOUSNESS OF OUR NATIONAL ENTITY

Paradoxical and extreme conceptions, such as socialism, anarchism, and communism, are all based in the final analysis on individualism, which is the root of modern Occidental ideologies and of which they are no more than varied manifestations. Yet even in the Occident, where individualism has formed the basis of their ideas, when it has come to communism, they have found it unacceptable; so that now they are about to do away with their traditional individualism, and this has led to the rise of totalitarianism and nationalism and to the springing up of Fascism and Nazism. That is, it can be said that both in the Occident and in our country the deadlock of individualism has led alike to a season of ideological and social confusion and crisis. . . . This means that the present conflict seen in our people's ideas, the unrest of their modes of life, the confused state of their civilization, can be put right only by a thorough investigation by us of the intrinsic nature of Occidental ideologies and by grasping the true meaning of our national polity. Then, too, this should be done not only for the sake of our nation but for the sake of the entire human race which is struggling to find a way out of the deadlock with which individualism is faced. . . .

LOYALTY AND PATRIOTISM

Our country is established with the emperor, who is a descendant of Amaterasu Ōmikami, as her center, and our ancestors as well as we ourselves constantly have beheld in the emperor the fountainhead of her life and activities. For this reason, to serve the emperor and to receive the emperor's great august Will as one's own is the rationale of making our historical "life" live in the present; and on this is based the morality of the people.

Loyalty means to reverence the emperor as [our] pivot and to follow him implicitly. By implicit obedience is meant casting ourselves aside and serving the emperor intently. To walk this Way of loyalty is the sole Way in which we subjects may "live," and the fountainhead of all energy. Hence, offering our lives for the sake of the emperor does not mean so-called self-sacrifice, but the casting aside of our little selves to live under his august grace and the enhancing of the genuine life of the people of a State. The relationship between the emperor and the subjects is not an artificial relationship [which means] bowing down to authority, nor a relationship such as [exists] between master and servant as is seen in feudal morals. . . . The ideology which interprets the relationship between the emperor and his subjects as being a reciprocal relationship such as merely [involves] obedience to authority or rights and duties, rests on individualistic ideologies, and is a rationalistic way of thinking that looks on everything as being in equal personal relationships. An individual is an existence belonging to a State and her history which forms the basis of his origin, and is fundamentally one body with it. . . .

From the point of individualistic personal relationships, the relationship between sovereign and subject in our country may [perhaps] be looked upon as that between non-personalities. However, this is nothing but an error arising from treating the individual as supreme, from the notion that has individual thoughts for its nucleus, and from personal abstract consciousness. Our relationship between sovereign and subject is by no means a shallow, horizontal relationship such as implies a correlation between ruler and citizen, but is a relationship springing from a basis transcending this correlation, and is that of "dying to self and returning to [the] One," in which this basis is not lost. This is a thing that can never be understood from an individualistic way of thinking. In our country, this great Way has seen a natural development since the founding of the nation, and the most basic thing that has manifested itself as regards the subjects is in short this Way of loyalty. . . .

FILIAL PIETY

In our country filial piety is a Way of the highest importance. Filial piety originates with one's family as its basis, and in its larger sense has the nation for its foundation. Filial piety directly has for its object one's parents, but in its relationship toward the emperor finds a place within loyalty.

The basis of the nation's livelihood is, as in the Occident, neither the individual nor husband and wife. It is the home. . . . A family is not a body of people established for profit, nor is it anything founded on such a thing as individual or correlative love. Founded on a natural relationship of begetting and being begotten, it has reverence and affection as its kernel; and is a place where everybody, from the very moment of his birth, is entrusted with his destiny.

The life of a family in our country is not confined to the present life of a household of parents and children, but beginning with the distant ancestors, is carried on eternally by the descendants. The present life of a family is a link between the past and the future, and while it carries over and develops the objectives of the ancestors, it hands them over to its descendants. . . .

Such things as [the carrying on of family traditions] show that the basis of the nation's life is in the family and that the family is the training ground for moral discipline based on natural sympathies. Thus, the life of a household is not a thing confined to the present, but is an unbroken chain that passes through from ancestor to offspring. . . .

The relationship between parent and child is a natural one, and therein springs the affection between parent and child. Parent and child are a continuation of one chain of life; and since parents are the source of the children, there spontaneously arises toward the children a tender feeling to foster them. Since children are extensions of parents, there springs a sense of respect, love for, and indebtedness toward, parents. . . .

LOYALTY AND FILIAL PIETY AS ONE

Filial piety in our country has its true characteristics in its perfect conformity with our national polity by heightening still further the relationship between morality and nature. Our country is a great family nation, and the Imperial Household is the head family of the subjects and the nucleus of national life. . . .

In China, too, importance is laid on filial duty, and they say that it is the source of a hundred deeds. In India, too, gratitude to parents is taught. But their filial piety is not of a kind related to or based on the nation. Filial piety is a characteristic of Oriental morals; and it is in its convergence with loyalty that we find a characteristic of our national morals, and this is a factor without parallel in the world. . . .

HARMONY

When we trace the marks of the facts of the founding of our country and the progress of our history, what we always find there is the spirit of harmony. Harmony is a product of the great achievements of the founding of the nation, and is the power behind our historical growth; it is also a humanitarian Way inseparable from our daily lives. The spirit of harmony is built on the concord of all things. When people determinedly count themselves as masters and assert their egos, there is nothing but contradictions and the setting of one against the other; and harmony is not begotten. In individualism it is possible to have cooperation, compromise, sacrifice, etc., so as to regulate and mitigate this contradiction and the setting of one against the other; but after all there exists no true harmony. That is, a society of individualism is one of clashes between [masses of] people . . . and all history may be looked upon as one of class wars. Social structure and political systems in such a society, and the theories of sociology, political science, statecraft, etc., which are their logical manifestations, are essentially different from those of our country which makes harmony its fundamental Way. . . .

Harmony as in our nation is a great harmony of individuals who, by giving play to their individual differences, and through difficulties, toil and labor, converge as one. Because of individual differences and difficulties, this harmony becomes all the greater and its substance rich. Again, in this way individualities are developed, special traits become beautiful, and at the same time they even enhance the development and well-being of the whole. . . .

THE MARTIAL SPIRIT

And then, this harmony is clearly seen also in our nation's martial spirit. Our nation is one that holds *bushidō* in high regard, and there are shrines deifying warlike spirits. . . . But this martial spirit is not [a thing that exists] for the sake of itself but for the sake of peace, and is what may

be called a sacred martial spirit. Our martial spirit does not have for its objective the killing of men, but the giving of life to men. This martial spirit is that which tries to give life to all things, and is not that which destroys. That is to say, it is a strife which has peace as its basis with a promise to raise and to develop; and it gives life to things through its strife. Here lies the martial spirit of our nation. War, in this sense, is not by any means intended for the destruction, overpowering, or subjugation of others; and it should be a thing for the bringing about of great harmony, that is, peace, doing the work of creation by following the Way. . . .

THE INHERENT CHARACTER OF THE [JAPANESE] PEOPLE

A pure, cloudless heart is a heart which, dying to one's ego and one's own ends, finds life in fundamentals and the true Way. That means, it is a heart that lives in the Way of unity between the Sovereign and his subjects, a Way that has come down to us ever since the founding of the empire. It is herein that there springs up a frame of mind, unclouded and right, that bids farewell to unwholesome self-interest. The spirit that sacrifices self and seeks life at the very fountainhead of things manifests itself eventually as patriotism and as a heart that casts self aside in order to serve the State. . . .

In the inherent character of our people there is strongly manifested alongside this spirit of self-effacement and disinterestedness, a spirit of broadmindedness and assimilation. In the importation of culture from the Asian Continent, too, in the process of "dying to self" and adopting the ideographs used in Chinese classics, this spirit of ours has coordinated and assimilated these same ideographs. To have brought forth a culture uniquely our own, in spite of the fact that a culture essentially different was imported, is due entirely to a mighty influence peculiar to our nation. This is a matter that must be taken into serious consideration in the adaptation of modern Occidental culture.

The spirit of self-effacement is not a mere denial of oneself, but means living to the great, true self by denying one's small self. . . .

BUSHIDŌ

Bushidō may be cited as showing an outstanding characteristic of our national morality. In the world of warriors one sees inherited the totalitarian structure and spirit of the ancient clans peculiar to our nation. Hence, though the teachings of Confucianism and Buddhism have been followed, these have been transcended. That is to say, though a sense of obligation binds master and servant, this has developed into a spirit of self-effacement and of meeting death with a perfect calmness. In this, it was not that death was made light of so much as that man tempered himself to death and in a true sense regarded it with esteem. In effect, man tried to fulfill true life by way of death. . . .

The warrior's aim should be, in ordinary times, to foster a spirit of reverence for the deities and his own ancestors in keeping with his family tradition; to train himself to be ready to cope with emergencies at all times; to clothe himself with wisdom, benevolence, and valor; to understand the meaning of mercy; and to strive to be sensitive to the frailty of Nature. . . . It is this same *bushidō* that shed itself of an outdated feudalism at the time of the Meiji Restoration, increased in splendor, became the Way of loyalty and patriotism, and has evolved before us as the spirit of the Imperial Forces. . . .

CONCLUSION

Every type of foreign ideology that has been imported into our country may have been quite natural in China, India, Europe, or America, in that it has sprung from their racial or historical characteristics; but in our country, which has a unique national polity, it is necessary as a preliminary step to put these types to rigid judgment and scrutiny so as to see if they are suitable to our national traits. . . .

To put it in a nutshell, while the strong points of Occidental learning and concepts lie in their analytical and intellectual qualities, the characteristics of Oriental learning and concepts lie in their intuitive and aesthetic qualities. These are natural tendencies that arise through racial and historical differences; and when we compare them with our national spirit, concepts, or mode of living, we cannot help recognizing further great and fundamental differences. Our nation has in the past imported, assimilated, and sublimated Chinese and Indian ideologies, and has therewith supported the Imperial Way, making possible the establishment of an original culture based on her national polity. . . .

Now, when we consider how modern Occidental ideologies have given birth to democracy, socialism, communism, anarchism, etc., we note, as already stated, the existence of historical backgrounds that form the bases of all these concepts, and, besides, the existence of individualistic views of life that lie at their very roots. The basic characteristics of modern Occidental cultures lie in the fact that an individual is looked upon as an existence of an absolutely independent being, all cultures comprising the perfection of this individual being who in turn is the creator and determiner of all values. Hence, value is laid on the subjective thoughts of an individual; the conception of a State, the planning of all systems, and the constructing of theories being solely based on ideas conceived in the individual's mind. The greater part of Occidental theories of State and political concepts so evolved do not view the State as being a nuclear existence that gives birth to individual beings, which it transcends, but as an expedient for the benefit, protection, and enhancement of the welfare of individual persons; so that these theories have become expressions of the principles of subsistence which have at their center free, equal, and independent individuals. As a result, there have arisen types of mistaken liberalism and democracy that have solely sought untrammeled freedom and forgotten moral freedom, which is service. Hence, wherever this individualism and its accompanying abstract concepts developed, concrete and historical national life became lost in the shadow of abstract theories; all states and peoples were looked upon alike as nations in general and as individuals in general; such things as an international community comprising the entire world and universal theories common to the entire world were given importance rather than concrete nations and their characteristic qualities; so that in the end there even arose the mistaken idea that international law constituted a higher norm than national law, that it stood higher in value, and that national laws were, if anything, subordinate to it.

The beginnings of modern Western free economy are seen in the expectation of bringing about national prosperity as a result of free, individual, lucrative activities. In the case of the introduction into our country of modern industrial organizations that had developed in the West, as long as the spirit striving for national profit and the people's welfare governed the people's mind, the lively and free individual activities went very far toward contributing to the nation's wealth; but later, with the dissemination of individualistic and liberal ideas, there gradually arose a tendency openly to justify egoism in economic management and operations. This tendency gave rise to the problem of a chasm between rich and poor, and finally became the cause of the rise of ideas of class war-

fare; while later the introduction of communism brought about the erroneous idea which looked upon economics as being the basis of politics, morality, and all other cultures, and which considered that by means of class warfare alone could an ideal society be realized. The fact that egoism and class warfare are opposed to our national polity needs no explanation. Only where the people one and all put heart and soul into their respective occupations, and there is coherence or order in each of their activities, with their minds set on guarding and maintaining the prosperity of the Imperial Throne, is it possible to see a healthy development in the people's economic life.

The same thing holds true in the case of education. Since the Meiji Restoration our nation has adapted the good elements of the advanced education seen among European and American nations, and has exerted efforts to set up an educational system and materials for teaching. The nation has also assimilated on a wide scale the scholarship of the West, not only in the fields of natural science, but of the mental sciences, and has thus striven to see progress made in our scholastic pursuits and to make education more popular. . . . However, at the same time, through the infiltration of individualistic concepts, both scholastic pursuits and education have tended to be taken up with a world in which the intellect alone mattered, and which was isolated from historical and actual life; so that both intellectual and moral culture drifted into tendencies in which the goal was the freedom of man, who had become an abstract being, and the perfecting of the individual man. At the same time, these scholastic pursuits and education fell into separate parts, so that they gradually lost their synthetic coherence and concreteness. In order to correct these tendencies, the only course open to us is to clarify the true nature of our national polity, which is at the very source of our education, and to strive to clear up individualistic and abstract ideas. . . .

In the Occident, too, many movements are now being engaged in to revise individualism. Socialism and communism, which are types of class individualism and which are the opposites of so-called bourgeois individualism, belong to these movements, while recent ideological movements, such as that called Fascism, which are types of nationalism and racial consciousness, also belong to this category. If, however, we sought to correct the evils brought about by individualism in our country and find a way out of the deadlock which it has created, it would not do to adopt such ideas as Occidental socialism and their abstract totalitarianism wholesale, or copy their concepts and plans, or [on the other hand] mechanically to exclude Occidental cultures.

OUR MISSION

Our present mission as a people is to build up a new Japanese culture by adopting and sublimating Western cultures without national polity as the basis, and to contribute spontaneously to the advancement of world culture. Our nation early saw the introduction of Chinese and Indian cultures, and even succeeded in evolving original creations and developments. This was made possible, indeed, by the profound and boundless nature of our national polity; so that the mission of the people to whom it is bequeathed is truly great in its historical significance. The call for a clarification of our national polity is at this time very much in the fore; but this must unfailingly be done by making the sublimation of Occidental ideologies and cultures its occasion, since, without this, the clarification of our national polity is apt to fall into abstractions isolated from actualities. That is to say, the adoption and sublimation of Occidental ideologies and the clarification of our national polity are so related as to be inseparable.

The attitude of the Japanese in the past toward the cultures of the world has been independent and yet at the same time comprehensive. Our contributions to the world lie only in giving full play more than ever to our Way which is of the Japanese people. The people must more than ever create and develop a new Japan by virtue of their immutable national polity which is the basis of the State and by virtue of the Way of the Empire which stands firm throughout the ages at Home and abroad, and thereby more than ever guard and maintain the prosperity of the Imperial Throne which is coeval with heaven and earth. This, indeed, is our mission.

Shinto Nationalism

D. C. HOLTOM

After the Meiji Restoration Japan's rulers made full use of the potentialities of the native Shinto religion to mobilize the people in the service of national goals. The Shinto-inspired form of nationalism became particularly strident in the 1930's. One of the foremost foreign authorities on the subject is D. C. Holtom, from whose book, *Modern Japan and Shinto Nationalism*, the following passages and quotations are taken. It should be remembered that Dr. Holtom is referring to the 1930's and early 1940's; State Shinto was disestablished after Japan's defeat in 1945.

T HE "divine edict" appears in the form of a commission laid on the grandson of the sun-goddess when she sent him down out of Takama-ga-Hara, the heaven of the old mythology, to take possession of the territory that was to become the new racial home on earth below . . .

This Reed-plain-1,500-autumns-fair-rice-ear Land [a rhetorical name for Japan] is the region which my descendants shall be lords of.

Do thou, my August Grandson, proceed thither and govern it. Go! and may prosperity attend thy dynasty, and may it, like Heaven and Earth, endure forever.

Dr. Shōzō Kōno, head of the Shinto College of Tokyo, the man who is chiefly responsible for the training of the Shinto priesthood, has said regarding these words:

This august message of the Imperial Ancestress has been looked upon by later generations as an expression of the Divine Will coexistent with heaven and earth. It is also considered as the fundamental faith of the nation and the motivating force of all activities. Furthermore, it is the source and foundation of Article I of the Japanese Constitution which reads, "The Empire of Japan shall be reigned over and governed by a line of Emperors unbroken for ages eternal."

The same authority says regarding the sun-goddess:

Then what is the essence or nature of Amaterasu-Ōmikami [the Sun Goddess]? It signifies the sublime and mightiest power of the nation, namely the Throne, and the great-august-heart or the soul of the ruler, which is embodied in the Throne. In other words, it represents the divine soul of the ruler of the empire, the Emperor. The Emperor is the divine manifestation of Amaterasu-Ōmikami and rules the empire in accordance with her will. Thus the Emperor and the Imperial Throne, transmitted in an unbroken line, are sacred and inviolable.

A person once called to the colors in Japan is summoned to participate in what can never be other than fundamentally and forever righteous. The sacred quality of the divine emperor attaches to a Japanese war. All the wars of Japan are holy wars since they are under the supreme com-

From D. C. Holtom, *Modern Japan and Shinto Nationalism*, pp. 53–54, 56, 64–65. (Chicago: University of Chicago Press).

mand of an emperor who can do nothing wrong. No matter how much the evil and crime with which an individual may have been defiled, it is all wiped away as soon as he has been placed under military command. We may translate directly at this point [from "The Imperial News," Sept. 18, 1938]:

No matter how much of a wrongdoer, no matter how evil, a Japanese subject may have been, when once he has taken his stand on the field of battle, all his past sins are entirely atoned for and they become as nothing. The wars of Japan are carried on in the name of the Emperor and therefore they are holy wars. All the soldiers who participate in these holy wars are representatives of the Emperor; they are his loyal subjects. To put the matter from the side of the subjects, we may say that every Japanese, regardless of what kind of person he may be, possesses the inherent capacity of becoming a loyal subject and of being empowered to put that loyalty into operation. The matchless superiority of the Japanese national life lies just here. . . .

Those who, with the words, "Tennō Heika Banzai" ["May the Emperor live forever"], on their lips, have consummated tragic death in battle, whether they are good or whether they are bad, are thereby sanctified.

The sanctification is thus twofold: it is by participation in a military cause that has been hallowed by the will of the sacred emperor and it is by a glorious death in his holy cause. From the person of the emperor emanates an influence that accomplishes atonement for sins. A national institution that presents to the members of the armed forces the prospect of joining the ranks of the sanctified *kami* [Shinto gods] through obedience to the sovereign and death in battle thus becomes the inspiration of the utmost devotion on the part of all those to whom genuine faith in these teachings is possible.

Amaterasu Ōmikami is thus, at one and the same time, the world-soul, the histori-cal Japanese manifestation of the world-soul, the racial head of the nation, the founder of the state, and the ancestress of the Imperial family. Contemporary Japan is . . . flooded with speculation of this sort. It is especially rife among the Shinto sects and has been worked into systems by philosophically minded individuals outside the sects who are seeking to give a speculative texture to the state religion. We may pause here for only a single example of the infra-rational depths to which these thinkers sometimes descend. I quote from Dr. Katsuhiko Kakehi, a prolific writer on Shinto and a former professor in the law school of the Imperial University of Toyko.

The primordial ancestor, offspring of the gods and herself a deity, was Amaterasu-Ōmikami, the Sun Goddess. The goddess everlastingly manifests Herself in the person of the Mikado, the August Ruler, the representative of the unbroken line of the Imperial Family, and in the firmament reigns supreme over the planetary system.

The last form of approach to the unfolding of the mysteries of Amaterasu Ōmikami is strictly historical. It utilizes the methodology of scientific study and comes to the conclusion that a sun myth is the key to the understanding of the original nature of the great goddess. This kind of investigation was possible in Japan twenty years ago. Today it finds itself guilty of lèse majesté.

In its actual functional value to modern Japan, the primitive solar mythology has been modified and enlarged by the influence of social and political patterns and impressed by the ulterior motives of tribal, dynastic, and racial aggrandizement, until, reshaped into its modern politico-religious mold, it becomes the symbol of the eternal state. As such, it is the central element of the national spirit, the chief ground for the belief in the one-tribe origin of the nation as all descended from a common ancestor, the inspiration of a spiritual mobilization program that is carried in a thousand ways to the length and breadth of the empire, a basis of unity and authority in human affairs that broadens its dominions over men with every success of Japanese arms, and the embodiment of the highest political authority elevated to the position of deity — in a word, the deification of the political might of the military state.

Agrarianism

MARUYAMA MASAO

Many writers in Japan and in the West have recognized agrarianism, or a stress on values and power based primarily on the land, as an outstanding characteristic of developments during the ultra-nationalist period. As we have seen, Tanin and Yohan consider that the importance of semi-feudal land-owners in Japan makes it impossible to regard the "reactionary chauvinist movement" in that country as fascist in the West European sense of the word. Although Professor Maruyama does not hesitate to use the term "fascist" to describe the dominant Japanese ideology during this period, he identifies certain distinctive points that are emphasized in the case of Japan. Of these the most important is the idea of agrarianism.

THERE is a tendency immanent in all "fascism" toward the strengthening of State authority and the exercise of a powerful control over all aspects of industry, culture and thought by means of a centralized State authority. But it is an important feature of Japanese "fascist" ideology that this tendency was checked by a counter-movement that demanded autonomy for villages in an attempt to put a stop to the expansion of the industrial productive power of the cities. Ōkawa Shūmei among rightists was the most deeply influenced by European education and culture. . . . Yet in the platform of the Society to Carry Out Heaven's Way on Earth, which he founded after breaking with Kita Ikki, we find the statement,

We must without question reject a capitalist economic policy which stresses commerce and industry in gross imitation of Western ways, and must establish a national economic policy according to agrarianism.

The platform also insists on "decentralization rather than centralization; local autonomy rather than a central Diet; the promotion of the villages rather than the predominance of the cities."

On the one hand, there is a tendency toward an ever greater strengthening of absolute State sovereignty focused on the Emperor; on the other, a tendency to centre the conception of Japan on provincial rather than on State affairs. In this respect the right wing may be divided into two sections: those who advocated an intensive development of industry and who wished to increase State control for this end, and those who flatly rejected the idea and thought in terms of agrarianism centred on the villages. Many members of the right wing held both these views, mingled in confusing eclecticism.

The purest representative of provincialism is perhaps Gondō Seikyō, who, after leaping into the limelight with the May 15 Incident, provided the ideological background of the Rural Self-Help Movement of 1932–33. His ideas as expressed in "Self-Government by the People" and "Treatise on Rural Self-Help" are thoroughly provin-

From Maruyama Masao, *Thought and Behaviour in Modern Japanese Politics*, Ivan Morris, ed., pp. 37–51 (London: Oxford University Press, 1963).

cial and even display an anti-nationalist outlook:

Generally speaking, there have since ancient times been two principles in the administration of States. One is to allow the people a life of autonomy, in which the sovereign hardly goes beyond setting examples, thereby giving the people a good standard. In the other the sovereign takes everything on himself and directs all State affairs. If the former may be termed the principle of autonomy, the latter may be termed *étatisme*. Japan was founded in complete accord with the former principle, and this was the ideal of all the ancient sages.

What is meant by *étatisme?* Its objectives are to mark out an area for a group called the State, to defend itself from external economic or military invasion, and to control other areas by means of its own economic and military power. In order to increase the prestige of the State, the mass of the people are treated as building materials and as machines to create public funds; all organizations are set up solely for administrative convenience, and the rulers exert enormous authority by controlling the masses through laws and ordinances. All public officials are given a privileged status; the spirit of sacrifice is made the supreme morality; and it becomes necessary to curb the expression of all thought. A detailed study reveals that *étatisme* and autonomy are of an entirely different nature.

The villages, having been sacrificed to this centralizing nationalism since the Meiji era, are now gasping in the nadir of stagnation and depression:

In the present state of fear and apprehension the villages suffer most. Our villages are the foundation of the country and the source of our habits and customs. At present the farmers form one half of our total population; they utilize the greater portion of the land; and they produce a large proportion not only of the staple foodstuffs of the nation, but also of its industrial raw materials and commercial goods.

However:
Tokyo and the other cities have expanded out of all proportion to the villages, and are replete with great buildings that are the last word in comfort and elegance. But, with the Great Depression, they are everywhere in financial difficulties. What is the reason for these widespread hardships?

After we have observed the present state of local autonomy, the drift of political party government and the morale of civil and military officials, it becomes perfectly clear that it is the impasse of bureaucratic government based on Prussian nationalism that has produced these abnormal phenomena.

I have quoted these passages in some detail because they most clearly represent the anti-official, anti-urban and anti-big-industry viewpoints in agrarianism.

The ideal State that Gondō Seikyō wished to establish was based on the native-village community in opposition to Prussian nationalism, and was a State structure built up from the bottom like a pyramid. Hence he upholds the conception of the "community" against the "nation." One feels that there is even a tinge of agrarian anarchism here. For example,

If the whole world became Japanese territory, the conception of the Japanese State would become unnecessary. But the conception of the community can never be discarded. The word "state" is used when one nation is opposed to another. It is a word representing divisions of the world map, and signifies the progressive formation of solidarity between villages, districts, cities and finally a country, in response to the need of men to live together. Even if all countries should remove their boundary lines, the conception of the community would not be destroyed as long as mankind exists.

This is an example of agrarianism pure and simple. Though it does not always go this far, the tendency against cities, industry and central authority is immanent to a greater or lesser extent in all Japanese "fascist" ideologies. Indeed this may be called a consistent tradition of the Japanist-nationalist movement since the Meiji era. Exactly the same thought appears in the Japanism of Miyake Setsurei and Shiga Jūkō, which in early 1887 was the first nationalist movement in modern Japan. For example, in an open letter to the Prime Minister, . . . Shiga . . . writes as follows:

There is only one thing we would ask of your administration. That is that the principle of preserving the national essence should be adopted as the national policy of Japan. . . . In this connection, although you are a man of affairs, we simply ask that when you go hunting with your dogs on official holidays or after work, you should get off at Hasuda or Koga stations and take a look at the wretched condition of the local inhabitants. You would then feel how all wealth and ability have been concentrated in Tokyo, how Tokyo has increasingly flourished and prospered while the localities have grown increasingly impoverished, as if Japan belonged to Tokyo and not Tokyo to Japan. Passing on to the seats of prefectural offices such as Utsunomiya and Fukushima, you will find that they are like smaller Tokyos, in which all the wealth and ability of the prefecture or province appears to be concentrated. Thus Japan is made up of one big Tokyo and scores of smaller Tokyos, without which it would not exist. Unfortunately the prosperity of Tokyo is in direct proportion to the decay of the countryside. Only when the people of all the provinces of a nation are rich can the nation as a whole be rich; only when the nation is rich can its army be strong. It is putting the cart before the horse to allow the strength of the inhabitants of the provinces to decline, and yet to hope to enrich the nation; or to try to strengthen the army without first enriching the country.

This is typical of the way in which early Japanese nationalists criticized the disparity in development between Tokyo and the provinces. In opposition to the Prussian nationalism of clan government, they advocated development of villages and cultivation of the strength of the people. The actual substance of the "Europeanization" that they attacked consisted of the rapid

establishment of capitalism by means of State authority from above, and it will be noted that their arguments correspond word for word with those of Gondō.

The development of Japanese capitalism was always attained at the sacrifice of agriculture; and the development of industry was lopsided, since capitalism developed by the concentration of specially favoured capital allied with State authority. Hence the thought that represented local interests left behind by this rapid central development came out consistently against modernization from above. The important point here is that this tradition eventually merged with "fascist" thought; in this respect their thinking provides an interesting comparison with that of the Narodniks in Tsarist Russia.

There are, of course, considerable variations in the degree to which rightists manifest this agrarianism. Kita Ikki's "General Outline of Measures for the Reconstruction of Japan" probably represents the palest colouring of the agrarian principle and is the most thoroughly based on centralized national control. His book advocated sweeping changes in governmental and economic organs centred on the authority of the Emperor, and can in fact be regarded as an expression of pure centralized authoritarianism. It includes suspension of the Constitution by the supreme authority of the Emperor; dissolution of the Diet; a *coup d'état* carried out by a national reconstruction Cabinet; restriction of individual private property to one million yen and confiscation of the surplus by the State; limitation of land ownership to a value of one hundred thousand yen; nationalization of enterprises with a capital of ten million yen or more, to be managed by Ministries for Banking, Navigation, Mining, Agriculture, Industry, Commerce and Railways. This work has the strongest colouring of centralized national socialism, and constitutes something of an exception in right-wing thought.

Tachibana Kōsaburō, who with Gondō Seikyō provided the ideology behind the May 15 Incident, speaks as follows in his "Principles of Japan's Patriotic Reformation."

According to a common expression, Tokyo is the hub of the world. But in my eyes it appears unhappily to be nothing but a branch shop of London. At all events, it is undeniable that the villages are being destroyed in direct proportion to the expansion of Tokyo. The farmers have never been so despised as now and the value of the villages has never been so disregarded.

Here we find the strong animosity against the centre and the cities which he shared with Gondō. Tachibana praises the life bound to the soil in the following words:

Man's world will be eternal so long as the bright sun is over his head and his feet are planted on the ground. Man's world will be peaceful so long as men remain brothers to one another. . . . What is tilling the soil if not the very basis of human life? It is a matter of fact that "everything that destroys the earth must also perish". . . . Only by agrarianism can a country become eternal, and that is especially the case with Japan. Neither in past, present nor future can Japan be herself if she is separated from the soil.

Tachibana thus displays a kind of Tolstoyan enthusiasm for the pastoral life. His position is not so thoroughly opposed to urban commerce and industry as that of Gondō, and he recognizes the merits of large-scale industry:

I do not say that large-scale industry and big business should be disregarded. I simply hold that, in view of the great objective of constructing a new Japan based on the principle of self-government, large-scale industry should be controlled and managed according to the principle of a welfare economy. At the same time I insist that we must not be thrown into that most dangerous of errors: the rash dream of immediately establishing a new so-

ciety and creating a new culture and a great revolution in world history merely by means of the expansion of large-scale industries and the application of their productive power to achieve the level of the most advanced nations.

This last point refers to Marxist socialism. In contrast, the ideal society advocated by Tachibana was a system of self-government and local autonomy based on the Kingly Way. As far as possible, production was to be controlled by popular co-operative organizations based on local jurisdiction. This may be called a compromise between the Kita Ikki and the Gondō Seikyō types. Such a compromising attitude was common in "fascism," and it is this point that makes its claims extremely illogical and fanciful.

For instance, the basic platform of the Great Japan Production Party declares:

The socialist reform policy attempts to establish a centralized socialist system in contradiction to a centralized capitalist system. They differ from each other only in so far as one is fused on capitalism and the other on socialism. Both are the same in being centralized systems. The policy of the Great Japan Production Party, on the other hand, aims at the autonomy principle. Autonomy does not mean rendering the central organ of the State completely powerless. While great importance is attached to State control, this will not require a strong centralized authority designed for the purpose. The excellence of the autonomy principle lies in this point. . . . Further, the Great Japan Production Party is flatly opposed to the anarchistic economic system of liberalism. Accordingly the Great Japan Production Party adopts the autonomy principle on the one hand, and on the other the principle of national control to the extent that it does not conflict with the former.

It is a confusing explanation; but in this respect too it is a typical "fascist" argument. Japanese "fascism" presents this confused appearance because the tendency toward the concentration of powerful authority and the strengthening of State control, which was common in world fascism, was limited in Japan by the ideology of agrarianism. It should be remembered, however, that the predominant position of this ideology in Japanese "fascism" did not rest simply on romanticism but was built on a definite social foundation.

As we have seen, the most important social cause for the sudden acceleration of the "fascist" movement in 1930–31 was that the world depression of 1929 caused above all a severe crisis in Japanese agriculture. The crisis that overtook capitalism in Japan naturally brought the heaviest pressure to bear upon the agricultural section of the economy, which was structurally the weakest. In the crop famine of 1930, the price of rice fell to 16 yen in October, and in June raw silk at 670 yen showed the lowest price since 1897. The terrible hardships of the farmers of northeast Japan as reported in the daily press are still fresh in one's memory. The extreme poverty of the villages forms the positive background for the acceleration of the "fascist" movement, and especially for the acts of right-wing terrorism that occurred continuously after 1931.

For instance, it is reported that just after the assassination of the Finance Minister, . . . Konuma Tadashi of the Blood Pledge Corps (which initiated this terrorism) told investigating officials, "The extremity of the villages is unbearable to see; it is the result of the bad policies of the former Finance Minister." In reporting the thought of the defendants after the May 15 Incident, the prosecution stated:

The political parties, the zaibatsu and a small privileged group attached to the ruling class are all sunk in corruption. They conspire in parties to pursue their own egoistic interests and desires, to the neglect of national defence and to the confusion of government. As a result national dignity is lost abroad, while at home the morale of the people collapses; the villages are exhausted, and medium and small industry and commerce have been driven to the wall.

Among domestic problems the exhaustion of the villages is given first place. That this was the direct motive which specially turned the young Army officers to radicalism is easily understandable in the light of the fact that many of these officers were the sons of lesser landowners or small independent cultivators. Moreover, the peasants, particularly those of the northeastern provinces, were regarded as the mainstay of the Army. Gotō Akinori, one of the Army defendants after the May 15 Incident, testified in court as follows:

The impoverishment of the farming villages is a cause of grave concern to all thoughtful people. It is the same with the fishing villages and the small merchants and industrialists. Among the troops the farmer conscripts make a good showing, and the farmers of the northeastern provinces provide the Army with model soldiers. It is extremely dangerous that such soldiers should be worried about their starving families when they are at the front exposing themselves to death. In utter disregard of poverty-stricken farmers the enormously rich zaibatsu pursue their private profit. Meanwhile the young children of the impoverished farmers of the northeastern provinces attend school without breakfast, and their families subsist on rotten potatoes. I thought that to let a day go by without doing anything was to endanger the Army for one day longer.

This statement amply demonstrates the social foundation of radical fascism. In the neat phrase of Tokutomi Sohō, "The farming villages were the electoral districts of the Army." The impoverishment of the villages thus gave a most important stimulus to Army interference in politics.

The prominence of agrarian ideology in Japanese "fascism" is, however, clearly contradictory to the realistic side of "fascism": the demand for the expansion of military production and the reorganization of the national economy round the armament industries. As "fascism" descends from the realm of ideas into the world of reality, agrarianism is bound to turn into an illusion. This was the fate of the right-wing ideology, particularly that of the military. For instance, in the sixty-ninth session of the Imperial Diet (May 1936), one of the members . . . made the following inquiry:

From the standpoint of national defense in a broad sense the necessity for a speedy solution to the problem of the villages is self-evident. We are quite willing to approve an increase in military expenditure so far as it is necessary to cope with the emergency. Indeed until now we have always given our approval. It is the result that concerns us. Since the manufacture of munitions depends largely on heavy industry, the funds expended for their manufacture flow mainly into industrial and commercial fields. This makes the armament industries flourish and brings about a lopsided prosperity, which results in the concentration of wealth and capital in the big cities and in the hands of big industrialists and merchants. In view of the expected future increase in the costs of national defence, unless steps are taken to remedy this concentration of wealth in the cities from military expenditure, its increase will result in the anomaly of even greater impoverishment of the villages and consequent injury to national defence in the broad sense. I should like a firm answer about whether the Army recognizes that military expenditure draws wealth and capital to the big cities and to the big industrialists and merchants and, if so, how they propose to correct this and promote the basis of national defence.

The War Minister, General Terauchi, replied as follows:

From the viewpoint of national defence in a broad sense, the Army is greatly concerned about the impoverishment of the villages. We admit that at present, owing to the location of barracks and armament factories, the disbursement of military expenditure tends to be made

in the cities. *We feel this to be unavoidable in the present state of industrial development.* In the disbursement of appropriated funds, however, the Army is doing its best in difficult conditions to give relief to the impoverished villages and to assist small and medium industries.

It was a rather lame reply. Despite the Army's wishful thinking, conditions grew progressively worse. As the armament industries developed, the burden fell more and more on the villages. The Army could not brush aside the practical problem of this excessive pressure on the villages, which supplied the best recruits. Patent uneasiness about this contradiction continued until the time of Tōjō. Much later, during the eighty-first session of the Diet (1943), the following question was put by . . . a member of the committee on the Bill for Special Regulations for Wartime Administration: "Are not the villages of Imperial Japan being endangered by the absorption of their labour power in the armament industries?" Premier Tōjō replied:

This is a point that truly worries me. On the one hand, I want at all costs to maintain the population of the villages at forty percent of the total population. I believe that the foundation of Japan lies in giving prime importance to agriculture. On the other hand, it is undeniable that industry is being expanded, chiefly because of the war. It is extremely hard to reconcile these two factors. However difficult it may be, I am determined to maintain the population of the villages at forty percent. But production must be increased. A harmony must be created by degrees between the two requirements. But, in creating this harmony, care must be taken to avoid making havoc of the Japanese family system. I must confess that things are not proceeding at present in an ideal manner. In the need for a rapid expansion of production large factories have been set up in various places; their workers have to be hired among the farmers, who naturally have to give up work on their farms. Although things are not proceeding ideally, I still believe that a method can and will be found to establish a proper harmony in the Japanese manner.

This anxious and pitiful answer reveals the contradiction between the structural characteristics of Japanese capitalism and the absolute necessity of increasing productive power. It also reveals the acute anxiety of the ruling class in the midst of the unprecedented turmoil of total war to preserve the village as the foundation of the Japanese family system. This is, of course, bound up with the problem of the traditional methods of agricultural enterprise. But the important point is that in the relentless march of history agrarian ideology as a positive force becomes an illusion, gradually receding from reality. On the other hand, it constantly acts as a check on government concern for the welfare facilities of the industrial workers.

This is an extremely important point, and it may well constitute the decisive difference between Japanese "fascism" and that of Nazi Germany. Of course, the Nazis also attached great importance to the farmers, as the expression *Blut und Boden* indicates; and they tried to bind them to the soil by such steps as the land inheritance law. But the Nazi Party was after all a "Workers' Party" (*Arbeitspartei*). The Nazis concentrated their energies on how to separate the working class from the power and influence of the social democratic and communist parties, and on how to convert them to Nazism. While the farmers formed one wing of the Nazi movement from the outset, it was extremely difficult to convert the organized workers to Nazism. The Nazis mobilized the industrial workers into *Arbeitsfronten* and took the greatest pains to get them to support Nazism by conciliatory measures such as *Kraft durch Freude*.

In the "fascist" ideology of Japan, however, the industrial workers were always slighted in comparison with the small and medium merchants and farmers. This was already so in the radical "fascist" movement, which came closer to representing the lower social stratum. The summation of the May 15 Incident mentions only "the exhaustion of the villages, the extreme poverty of small and medium shopkeepers and owners of small factories." No reference is made to the industrial workers. The pamphlet entitled "The True Meaning of National Defence: Its Consolidation Advocated," published by the War Ministry in October 1934, displays the typical military ideology of the second period. This is the pamphlet that begins with the famous sentence, "War is the father of creation and the mother of culture," and that became such a great issue in the Diet. It declares: "At present the most pressing problem of national welfare is to give relief to the farming, mountain and fishing villages." It presents the problem under the heading, "City versus Village." Of course, this does not mean that the authors of such pamphlets purposely made no reference to the industrial workers. When they spoke of the poverty and distress of the life of the people, they must have included the industrial working class in their thoughts. But the fact that they all discuss only the farmers and the small and medium shopkeepers and factory-owners reveals the insignificant place occupied by the industrial proletariat in their minds.

The notebook of Muranaka Kōji, a leader of the February Incident, states:

It must be realized that the Shōwa Restoration cannot be brought about until the military clique and the bureaucrats are crushed by the power of the common soldiers, the farmers and the workers.

A specific reference of this kind to the concrete agents of change is unusual in nationalist writings; yet it will be noticed that even here the industrial workers are put in last place. In the world of "fascist" ideas this was already so. Indeed in actual practice this tendency is far more openly displayed. It is well known that during the war the welfare facilities of the workers were far inferior even to those of the Nazis.

Japanese "fascist" leaders consistently harboured a deep-rooted pessimism regarding the value of industrial workers and the possibility of their spiritual and physical improvement. For example, during a committee meeting on the Bill for Special Regulations for Wartime Administration in the eighty-first session of the Diet (1942–43), Mr. Kawakami Jōtarō made the following inquiry:

I do not deny that the villages are a source of sturdy soldiers. However, if the factories are incapable of supplying sturdy soldiers, this is a defect and must be remedied. In the past the villages and the cities have been opposed to each other. I think it necessary that measures should henceforth be taken to do away with this opposition and to enable the factories as well as the villages to supply sturdy soldiers.

In a lengthy answer Tōjō replied,

Ideally, both the villages and the factories should be sources of sturdy soldiers. But I must say with regret that at present the factory workers are inferior to the men from the villages in everything, not only in physique. I may arouse anger by saying this, but it is an incontestable fact that farm workers are of firmer character. To that extent, the factory workers are inferior in present circumstances. . . . In short, I agree with your view that both the villages and the factories should supply sturdy soldiers and that our policies should be aimed at this objective. I should like to proceed in this direction, but I think that at present there is regrettably a great discrepancy between them.

A pessimistic view of the industrial workers runs consistently through this answer, demonstrating how agrarian ideology put a brake on a positive policy that would accept the factory workers. From this ensued the ill treatment of the drafted factory workers, their surprisingly poor lodgings and pay, and the indifference of the authorities to their situation. The result was a large-scale demoralization. The authorities then tried to remedy the situation by a combination of abstract "pep talks" and severe punishments.

The divergence between Japanese and German "fascism" in this respect is clearly revealed in the difference between Japan's Serve-the-State-through-Industry Movement and Nazi Germany's *Kraft durch Freude* movement. This does not mean that the Nazis had the independence and initiative of the workers at heart; in giving them holidays and sending them on coach trips once a year, their object was to divert the workers' attention from oppressive reality. Nevertheless in its careful consideration of the workers and in its welfare measures German "fascism" cannot be compared with the Japanese version. Of course this is also connected with the degree of capital accumulation in the two countries. But an important factor was that in the case of the Japanese factory workers there was no strong feeling that one would have liked to improve their conditions if only the materials had been available. Such coarse treatment was regarded as justified especially when it applied to drafted factory workers. Although this certainly reflects agrarian ideology, it must be noted that agrarianism alone did not bring about such a result. More fundamentally the cause lay in the difference between the strength of the proletariat in the two countries. The strength of the democratic movement prior to the "fascist" structure determined the extent of democratic trappings within "fascism." In the case of the Nazis the experience of the November Revolution and the baptism of Weimar democracy made their case decidedly different from that of Japan.

The Need for Emigration and Expansion

HASHIMOTO KINGORŌ

The aspect of Japanese ultra-nationalism that most directly (and painfully) affected other countries was its stress on a national destiny viewed in terms of world power (as epitomized in the slogan, "the eight corners of the world under one roof") and in particular on Japan's mission to promote pan-Asianism. The following selections will suggest in what ways these goals, and the justifications for them, were similar to expansionist ambitions in the West (e.g. to Hitler's demand for *Lebensraum*) and how they were characteristically Japanese.

WE have already said that there are only three ways left to Japan to escape from the pressure of surplus population. We are like a great crowd of people packed into a small and narrow room, and there are only three doors through which we might escape, namely emigration, advance into world markets, and expansion of territory. The first door, emigration, has been barred to us by the anti-Japanese immigration policies of other countries. The second door, advance into world markets, is being pushed shut by tariff barriers and the abrogation of commercial treaties. What should Japan do when two of the three doors have been closed against her?

It is quite natural that Japan should rush upon the last remaining door.

It may sound dangerous when we speak of territorial expansion, but the territorial expansion of which we speak does not in any sense of the word involve the occupation of the possessions of other countries, the planting of the Japanese flag thereon, and the declaration of their annexation to Japan. It is just that since the Powers have suppressed the circulation of Japanese materials and merchandise abroad, we are looking for some place overseas where Japanese capital, Japanese skills and Japanese labor can have free play, free from the oppression of the white race.

We would be satisfied with just this much. What moral right do the world powers who have themselves closed to us the two doors of emigration and advance into world markets have to criticize Japan's attempt to rush out of the third and last door?

If they do not approve of this, they should open the doors which they have closed against us and permit the free movement overseas of Japanese emigrants and merchandise. . . .

At the time of the Manchurian incident, the entire world joined in criticism of Japan. They said that Japan was an untrustworthy nation. They said that she had recklessly brought cannon and machine guns into Manchuria, which was the territory of another country, flown airplanes over it, and finally occupied it. But the military action taken by Japan was not in the least a selfish one. Moreover, we do not

From Ryusaku Tsunoda, Wm. Theodore de Bary, and Donald Keene, compilers, *Sources of the Japanese Tradition* pp. 796–98 (New York: Columbia University Press).

recall ever having taken so much as an inch of territory belonging to another nation. The result of this incident was the establishment of the splendid new nation of Manchuria. The Powers are still discussing whether or not to recognize this new nation, but regardless of whether or not other nations recognize her, the Manchurian empire has already been established, and now, seven years after its creation, the empire is further consolidating its foundations with the aid of its friend, Japan.

And if it is still protested that our actions in Manchuria were excessively violent, we may wish to ask the white race just which country it was that sent warships and troops to India, South Africa, and Australia and slaughtered innocent natives, bound their hands and feet with iron chains, lashed their backs with iron whips, proclaimed these territories as their own, and still continues to hold them to this very day?

They will invariably reply, these were all lands inhabited by untamed savages. These people did not know how to develop the abundant resources of their land for the benefit of mankind. Therefore it was the wish of God, who created heaven and earth for mankind, for us to develop these undeveloped lands and to promote the happiness of mankind in their stead. God wills it.

This is quite a convenient argument for them. Let us take it at face value. Then there is another question that we must ask them.

Suppose that there is still on this earth land endowed with abundant natural resources that have not been developed at all by the white race. Would it not then be God's will and the will of Providence that Japan go there and develop those resources for the benefit of mankind?

And there still remain many such lands on this earth.

The Spirit and Destiny of Japan

ARAKI SADAO

INTRODUCTION

As the result of his great expedition the founder of the Imperial Dynasty of Jinmu built the first Imperial Palace in Kawasibara, district of Yamato (now the Nara prefecture), and solemnly established the foundation of the state and the principle of Supreme Power.

Since then the Imperial line has continued uninterruptedly for 124 generations and the foundations of the state have become stronger from year to year. The great cause of the Japanese people (the people of Yamato) prospers from year to year under the fatherly guidance of the succeeding Emperors.

With deep emotion and pride we recall the brilliant 3,000-year history of the state. Especially under the Emperor Meiji, who took upon himself the great task of guiding the people of the newly established state, the people whose fame thunders over the entire globe — has the national spirit, long in a condition of latency, finally shown itself in all its activity and vital energy.

The Imperial State — Japan, rising so majestically over the clouds of the city of Fuji — has become a great figure in the world. Standing before this figure we cannot but feel even more proud and stimulated.

Lately, however, part of the people of Japan have forgotten the essentials of their own national spirit and the spirit of our system of government. They are easily penetrated by a frivolous foreign ideology and a tendency towards a transient merriment becomes more and more noticeable amongst them. Moreover, with every year there is a gradual extinction of the characteristic peculiarities of the Japanese people: simplicity, bravery, etc.

Such a condition is unquestionably the result of insufficient understanding and of foolishness. The process of deterioration of the national spirit is proceeding rapidly and it is very difficult to bring it back to the path of virtue. The silence maintained by authoritative people is so much more criminal at a time when they hear curses directed at the glorious state even though it be on the part of a small number of people.

We do not in the least doubt the sincerity of the Japanese people with its 3,000-year-old history, or in the righteousness of the foundations of our state, which must be eternal, like heaven and earth. But we must always follow the precept: "Be ready for the very worst and do everything possible to avoid that worst."

Expressing here my opinion on the problems facing Japan in the Era of Showa, I do not intend by this to make any radical changes. I am only thinking of the benefit it may bring even in a small degree.

ERRONEOUS PHILOSOPHY OF THE ABSENCE OF DIFFERENCES

The Buddhists preach: "Nature knows no differences." According to them where there are no differences there exists the so-called "true light." But this "true light" means "empty light," i.e., "light of nihil-

From O. Tanin and E. Yohan, *Militarism and Fascism in Japan* (New York: International Publishers, 1934), pp. 297–309.

66

ism." But is nihilism the essence of modernity? In other words can nihilism exist in a limited light? From this point of view the correctness of the philosophy of the absence of differences is subject to great doubt.

In reality nothing exists in the universe which has not its purpose: the sun, the moon, the countless stars, the globe — all have their definite purpose. This can also be said of our world: just as man has his characteristic human traits and peculiarities so has every animal and every plant its properties.

Only where there are differences there is merit.

Considering it superfluous here to compare man to animals let us take, for example, a dog. Take a pointer and a poodle. Both are dogs. But there is a big difference between them: while the poodle is valued only for amusement, the pointer helps in hunting and guarding. But if we place the pointer and poodle for several generations in the same conditions of training, surroundings, food, etc., the difference in their properties will disappear.

We have the same thing in the human world. If there is no great difference between people with respect to externals, there are nevertheless differences due to race and nationality.

We Japanese have our peculiarities and our purpose, and the Chinese have their peculiarities. There are such differences also among other states. Only when the peoples of different countries will know their own peculiarities and honestly try to attain their own purposes, only then will we have heaven on earth.

That is why we Japanese must have an adequate idea of our peculiarities and purposes and direct our activities accordingly. We cannot recognize the theory of the absence of differences. We believe that only by taking the point of view of absolute difference shall we come to a humanity where

there will exist no differences. There is no other way for us to follow.

REALIZATION OF ONESELF AS A JAPANESE

The present international situation causes much disquietude due to the open antagonisms among countries, the oppression of the weak by the more powerful, and the world economic crisis which brings the economies of various countries to a chaotic condition.

On the other hand within the country there are still some frivolous expressions of egoistical foreign ideas, which increase public disquietude.

The present time, pregnant with various sorts of events, has brought us face to face with an unwontedly serious situation. What should be our attitude to this situation?

That we must be cheerful — that goes without saying. But cheerfulness alone is not enough. We must first of all have a perspicacious "consciousness." Before undertaking a series of steps of an interior and exterior nature, they must be thoroughly investigated first. This makes the knowledge of ourselves the more urgent.

But by knowing ourselves we cannot yet take the proper steps. The fundamental thing is that everything must come from ourselves. If we forget this fundamental indispensable condition we shall unconsciously fall victims of illusions or heresy. It is for this reason we must say openly: "every study must begin with self-realization." Before beginning the study of one question or another under such unwontedly difficult circumstances we must firmly realize: "I am — a Japanese." To study any question without self-realization — is to measure without a measure.

Let us take one example — the present Manchurian situation. Why did the Manchurian events arise and what is their significance? — this the entire people must understand.

When the question is raised as to the causes of the Manchurian incident, every Japanese seeks these causes in the lawless violation of treaties by the Chinese, in the impermissible ignoring by the Chinese of international usages and their unjust infringements upon the rights and interests acquired by Japan.

It is indisputable that all these were reasons for the arising of the incident, but, frankly speaking, this incident did not grow out of such trivial questions. At the basis of it there is a fundamental question. And what is that? It is — that China has insulted Japan.

However, it may be said that not only China, but almost the entire world looks slightingly at Japan in its present situation.

What was China's position soon after the occurrence of the Manchurian incident? The sentiment of a number of governments, members of the League of Nations, is characteristically against Japan in connection with this incident!

In China treaties that should be strictly observed according to international public law are arbitrarily disregarded. The lawfully acquired rights and interests of Japan are continually infringed upon there. In addition such anti-Japanese activities have developed there that even in textbooks of elementary schools they write only against Japan. It is perfectly evident that sooner or later Japan had to lose its patience.

The action of Japan does not in any way contradict the principles of justice.

Having forgotten its fundamental task — to act on the basis of justice, the League of Nations for a long time has attempted to reject and condemn the just demands and actions of Japan. In the end it became clear that slighting Japan has become a strong tendency on a world scale.

To the question how such a situation occurred, the answer is simple. It occurred because the Japanese themselves had forgotten their national pride, forgotten their convictions and lost their self-realization. It occurred because the Japanese were sunk in frivolous foreign ideology, lowering their prestige before the whole world. It was therefore only natural that they found themselves insulted by a number of powers and China.

Hence, not only in order to work out protective measures with respect to Manchuria and Mongolia, but also to show the world our brilliant essence, it is necessary for us that the entire nation be awakened to the convictions and ideals of the Imperial Army so that the people will have the determination to go in for ever bigger aims avoiding individual pragmatic ideas.

For otherwise, even if and when the Manchuro-Mongolian question will be solved satisfactorily to Japan, the question will arise before us: will this situation last long?

A considerable section of the people is satisfied with the conversion of Manchuria and Mongolia into a Japanese colony only in an economic sense. But I am certain that out of such thoughtlessness we not only can expect nothing, but even in the very near future we shall be faced with events of a larger scale and significance than the present ones.

From this point of view it seems to us that the continental theory which up to now prevailed in Japan will prove an empty one.

We think that in considering and establishing the Japanese policy with regard to the continent, personal interests must be relegated to second place. The Japanese continental policy must aim higher. The economic development of Japan in Manchuria and Mongolia are in the end only of secondary importance. Inasmuch as development on the continent is necessary for the safety of Japan, for the safety of the East and for the safety of the world, we now need extreme determination.

But for this one must first of all have the self-realization: "I am — a Japanese."

THOUGHTS ON THE SPIRIT OF JAPAN

The secret of victory in war is knowledge of oneself and one's adversary. This is a basic principle which applies to everything. Without knowing oneself, one can know nothing.

I think that for Japan to get out of the present difficult situation there is no other means than that the entire Japanese people decidedly and fully realize they are Japanese. Only then will the development of Japan get its full swing when this self-realization is achieved.

But what must be the concrete object of such self-realization by the Japanese? What is the fundamental distinguishing trait of Japan? This is nothing but the great ideal, represented by the three regalias of the Japanese dynasty: Jasper, a mirror and a sword which were the presents of Amaterasuomikami at the creation of the Japanese state. As every Japanese knows these three regalias are the symbols:

> the mirror — of justice
> the jasper — of mercy
> the sword — of bravery

It is justice, mercy and bravery, represented by the regalias of the Japanese dynasty that are the fundamental ideals of the Japanese state, the way marked out by the Emperors. This is the so-called real "Imperial Course." Japanese history represents nothing but the realization of this course. To preserve this course, make it a glorious one, is the duty of the Japanese people as loyal subjects of His Majesty.

The fundamental essence of the Japanese system of government is the unity of high and low, of the Monarch and his people. This points clearly to the aim of the Japanese, which amounts to the glorification of the Emperor, for which purpose public welfare must take precedence over private, personal welfare.

And then, when the Japanese people will master this genuinely national spirit and realize its true purpose, it will naturally follow that it will strengthen its own development.

The present difficult situation cannot be overcome until the Japanese people will be inspired with the desire to realize with maximum determination its great ideal of world significance. Without this inspiration it is impossible either to solve the Manchuro-Mongolian problem or that of continental policy.

All this is confirmed by such historical facts as took place beginning with the Meiji Era, like the Japanese-Chinese, the Japano-Russian and the Japano-German wars, solemnly conducted under this great ideal. Japan's position was then acknowledged by the whole world. On this basis arose the greatness of the Japanese state and its power grew and strengthened. If these wars had been conducted by Japan on the basis of egoistic interest, if they had been of a predatory plundering character, then Japan would in all probability have been the subject of reproach on the part of all the governments of the world and would finally have found itself in a difficult position, bordering on an impasse. Germany during the recent European war was a living example of this.

From the very beginning of history Japanese superiority consisted in this, that evil and injustice never guided its actions, never took the place of high virtue in its deeds.

Now there is, however, a basis for disquietude, as there are groups among the people, though few in number, but who taken in by foreign radical ideology and following Marxian theories sometimes forget the honor of Japan, its aims and their duty. There are also people that are conducting themselves in a way which leads to ruin, as they give themselves over to slothfulness and rest while lacking ideals and consciousness.

It is unnecessary to speak here of the fact that the theory of materialism that does not recognize the spiritual functions of man, transforming him into a machine, robbing him of his ideals and freedom, transforming him into a public slave — is harmful for a healthy society.

We, who believe in Japanese traditions and the Japanese spirit, strongly desire that the entire Japanese people quickly awake from their evil sleep and, united under the great ideal, become the preacher-apostle of high Imperial virtue.

JAPAN AND PEACE

Now let us consider the external position of Japan.

Since Japan, beginning with the Meiji Era, has shown the whole world its real, sincere face, it has always acted on the basis of justice and had the determination to resort to real force, sacrificing itself for the benefit of the world. It never hesitated in the matter of the annihilation of evil. As a result it has become one of the three greatest powers of the world.

To give support to the greatness of the Emperor means to realize the great ideal of Great Japan. For this purpose the Japanese people gathered all its forces as it burned with the great self-realization as the Japanese people.

However, lately, this strong national enthusiasm is gradually waning, it can even be said it is in a severely fallen state.

As an example, we shall take the spread of frivolous ideology in society. Capitalists are concerned only with their own interests and pay no attention to public life; politicians often forget the general situation in the country while absorbed in their party interests; clerks and students forget their duty giving themselves over to merriment and pleasures.

In a word, it can be said that there is frivolity everywhere, egoism replacing cheerfulness, honor and ideals. Who can fail to be disquieted about the future of the state when thinking over the further results of such a situation? And this is not only a question of the future. Signs of disaster are already adumbrated.

In reality we have the important sad fact of the isolation of Japan in its international position — and the Japanese people must know that until they will not abandon their indifference, Japan will always be subject to such a position of isolation.

It is necessary to study the causes of this without delay. They consist in this — that the Japanese have forgotten their national self-realization, forgotten the correct understanding of Imperial Japan.

What can remain of Japan when the great soul of the state is forgotten, when national pride is abandoned? The fact that Japan is now an object of disdain on the part of the entire world and has been insulted by China is in the long run the fault of Japan itself. It must be well understood that this is the origin of the Manchurian incident as well as the attack on Japan on the part of the governments united in the League of Nations.

I repeat, the present Manchurian incident arose not on the basis of such trivial questions as the ignoring of treaty obligations or the infringement of the rights and interests of Japan. The fundamental reason for the incident is the insult of Japan by China. The League of Nations could not distinguish between justice and injustice which brought about the result that it too insults Japan. It must thus be evident to everybody that the direct cause of Japanese isolation lies in the insult received by it from all the world and that this happened by the fault of Japan itself.

The Japanese people must understand this clearly. It must also understand that only by mastering this truth can it get out of the present difficulties.

In the face of such a situation the Manchurian incident is for Japan a sign of God. It must be admitted that God has given the alarm in order to awaken the Japanese people.

We are by no means pessimistic with regard to the present difficult situation. We firmly believe that the present international situation will rapidly improve for Japan if the Japanese people will be regenerated with the great soul of the Japanese state and show itself as the Japanese people. On this condition the time will soon come when the entire world will joyously welcome Imperial virtue.

THE PRESENT POSITION OF EASTERN ASIA

Our "Imperial virtue" which is the embodiment of the union between the true soul of the Japanese state and the great ideal of the Japanese people, must be preached and spread over the whole world. All obstacles interfering with this must be destroyed with strong determination not stopping at the application of real force.

Here we must first analyze the present situation in Eastern Asia, as the measures taken by us are determined primarily by the conditions of the countries which are our immediate neighbors.

Question: what is the situation in Eastern Asia at the present time?

In China there has been a continuous reign of disorder for the past twenty years, and to this very date there is not even a central government in existence nor the very essence of government.

In India more than 300,000,000 people suffer under English oppression and it now stands face to face with a serious crisis.

As in Central Asia so also in Siberia there is not a shred of liberty. And Mongolia has also, it would seem, become another Central Asia. Thus on the continent of Eastern Asia the only other independent state besides Japan is Siam.

Under such circumstances it is impossible to remain silent and lose sight of Japan which is the strongest state in Eastern Asia and which not only has the corresponding real force but also the historic mission to save a number of states of Eastern Asia. Japan must rise determinedly in the name of justice even if it really threatened the ruin of our homeland. In any event we must fight determinedly for the truth.

It is said that England is a country of gentlemen. If that is so why is the national-liberation movement in India growing sharper from year to year? In America the emblem of humanity and justice is flaunted, but are they felt with respect to its foreign policy towards Panama, Cuba, Mexico and a number of countries of Central and South America? On investigating other countries active on the international arena we see that nowhere is Imperial virtue to be found.

Different countries in Eastern Asia are the objects of oppression on the part of the white race.

Awakened Imperial Japan can no longer tolerate the arbitrariness of the white race. It is the Japanese mission to struggle against all acts incompatible with Imperial virtue no matter what country is responsible for such acts.

In this respect Japan cannot overlook a single instance of disorder springing up anywhere in Eastern Asia. As the infringement of peace is absolutely incompatible with the great ideals of Imperial Japan, we must always be adequately prepared and have the determination to remove such disorders at once even if it be necessary to resort to real force for this purpose. We are certain that so long as we have such determination and the real force we can expect peace.

We are exceedingly sorry that China does not yet understand the sincerity of Japan and resorts in vain to the assistance of Europe and America, that it still continues the game of technical diplomacy, getting from year to year into a less advantageous position.

It is a superficial view or a conscious distortion of reality to imagine that Japan is a militaristic country and conducts an aggressive policy. Japan has no other intentions than to realize with all its power the fundamental ideal — the preservation of peace.

In the Manchurian incident Japan resorted to force of arms. But this means that Japan has taken up the sword in order to save many by sacrificing one. . . .

THE QUESTION OF THE KOREANS

To maintain peace in the East — this is a traditional state principle of Imperial Japan. It proved it numerous times at the risk of its own fate. Japan conducted the Japano-Chinese, the Japano-Russian and Japano-German wars only for the purpose of primarily maintaining peace in the Far East.

We repeat: maintaining peace in the Far East means first of all the spread of Imperial virtue. From this follow all internal and external measures adopted by Japan. On this was also based the annexation of Korea by Japan. We feel very sorry that in the course of time the truth is being forgotten. In the Imperial edict on the annexation of Korea it says:

Under my grace the masses of the people will increase their welfare. Industry and trade will develop materially under conditions of quiet times. I am firmly convinced that by this the cause of peace in the Far East will be strengthened.

Of the greatness of the soul of the previous Emperor Meiji one can judge from the quoted words. But did the succeeding statesmen pay good heed to these words?

Thanks to a number of steps the welfare of Korea is increasing every day and every month. But one important fact was left out of view — the question of the Koreans living in Manchuria. They have long been subjects of the Emperor and our compatriots. Regardless of the fact that there are 800,000 of them, their existence has up to now not been taken into account. Under the oppression of the beastly Chinese powers their life and property was always in danger.

About what does this fact make us think? Having before us masses of millions tramping about in search of land, we cannot but take upon ourselves the responsibility for leaving them in this state.

The full union of Korea and Japan is the foundation of peace in the Far East. We cannot fail to take care of the Koreans. They must be fed, given strength to live and thus secure their future. Otherwise the great spirit of the annexation of Korea will finally perish.

It would be a great mistake to think that in obtaining concessions for railroads and mines the aims of the Manchuro-Mongolian policy of Japan are fully accomplished. Up to now Japan, concentrating attention on these rights and interests, has aroused the suspicion of other countries and found itself isolated. Utilizing the present incident we must show by our actions that the declarations and deeds of Japan originate wholly in the principle of humanity and in aiming for peace.

Further, in the eastern part of Siberia several hundred thousand Koreans live and their situation is even more terrible. We must feel deeply the necessity to take care of them as we do with respect to those Koreans that live in Manchuria and take the necessary measures to help them in the near future. Our traditions and national feelings do not permit us to silently, with folded hands, observe their terrible plight.

JAPANESE — APOSTLES OF PEACE

From the beginning of history Japan has been "a country of the military arts." However, together with this a tradition has existed not to take up arms arbitrarily. In this lay the national prestige of Japan and that is why Japan never took up arms arbitrarily. Thus it firmly carries out the spirit of the Imperial Army whose course rests on justice and mercy.

It is entirely superficial to consider Japan a militaristic or imperialistic country. Such an idea only he can have who does not know that Japan takes up arms only in the struggle for peace.

Of how Japan loves peace and aspires to quiet and the welfare of man one can judge from the Imperial edicts of every Emperor where this is clearly stated. Japan respects military art only for the purpose of realizing its great ideals.

The Japanese people must not adopt uncritically American and European culture and weaken the traditional spirit of Japan.

Developing its great spirit that has defined itself for 3,000 years, the Japanese people must strive to spread Imperial virtue. In this lies its eternal life and fame as an apostle of peace.

Down with the heretical doctrine of materialism! Destroy vicious tendencies!

One must not rely on matter.

A strong spirit and cheerfulness, in the end, decide everything.

The question of the size of the population is important. The supply question is important. The question of the international situation is, of course, important. But we must not disquiet ourselves too much about these questions. The Japanese people must rise above all others and look further than others. When it will realize its mission and its purpose all these problems will solve themselves.

The Way of Japan and the Japanese

ŌKAWA SHŪMEI

ASIA's stubborn efforts to remain faithful to spiritual values, and Europe's honest and rigorous speculative thought, are both worthy of admiration, and both have made miraculous achievements. Yet today it is no longer possible for these two to exist apart from each other. The way of Asia and the way of Europe have both been traveled to the end. World history shows us that these two must be united; when we look at that history up to now we see that this unification is being achieved only through war. Mohammed said that "Heaven lies in the shadow of the sword," and I am afraid that a struggle between the great powers of the East and the West which will decide their existence is at present, as in the past, absolutely inevitable if a new world is to come about. The words "East-West struggle," however, simply state a concept and it does not follow from this that a united Asia will be pitted against a united Europe. Actually there will be one country acting as the champion of Asia and one country acting as the champion of Europe, and it is these who must fight in order that a new world may be realized. It is my belief that Heaven has decided on Japan as its choice for the champion of the East. Has not this been the purpose of our three thousand long years of preparation? It must be said that this is a truly grand and magnificent mission. We must develop a strong spirit of morality in order to carry out this solemn mission, and realize that spirit in the life of the individual and of the nation.

From Ryusaku Tsunoda, Wm. Theodore de Bary, and Donald Keene, compilers, *Sources of the Japanese Tradition*, pp. 795–96 (New York: Columbia University Press).

Draft of Basic Plan for Establishment of Greater East Asia Co-Prosperity Sphere

The Plan. The Japanese empire is a manifestation of morality and its special characteristic is the propagation of the Imperial Way. It strives but for the achievement of *Hakkō Ichiu*,[1] the spirit of its founding. . . . It is necessary to foster the increased power of the empire, to cause East Asia to return to its original form of independence and co-prosperity by shaking off the yoke of Europe and America, and to let its countries and peoples develop their respective abilities in peaceful cooperation and secure livelihood.

The Form of East Asiatic Independence and Co-Prosperity. The states, their citizens, and resources, comprised in those areas pertaining to the Pacific, Central Asia, and the Indian Oceans formed into one general union are to be established as an autonomous zone of peaceful living and common prosperity on behalf of the peoples of the nations of East Asia. The area including Japan, Manchuria, North China, lower Yangtze River, and the Russian Maritime Province, forms the nucleus of the East Asiatic Union. The Japanese empire possesses a duty as the leader of the East Asiatic Union.

The above purpose presupposes the inevitable emancipation or independence of Eastern Siberia, China, Indo-China, the South Seas, Australia, and India.

Regional Division in the East Asiatic Union and the National Defense Sphere

[1] "The eight corners of the world under one roof" — see Glossary. [Editor's note]

for the Japanese Empire. In the Union of East Asia, the Japanese empire is at once the stabilizing power and the leading influence. To enable the empire actually to become the central influence in East Asia, the first necessity is the consolidation of the inner belt of East Asia; and the East Asiatic Sphere shall be divided as follows for this purpose:

The Inner Sphere—the vital sphere for the empire — includes Japan, Manchuria, North China, the lower Yangtze Area and the Russian Maritime area.

The Smaller Co-Prosperity Sphere — the smaller self-supplying sphere of East Asia — includes the inner sphere plus Eastern Siberia, China, Indo-China and the South Seas.

The Greater Co-Prosperity Sphere — the larger self-supplying sphere of East Asia — includes the smaller co-prosperity sphere, plus Australia, India, and island groups in the Pacific. . . .

For the present, the smaller co-prosperity sphere shall be the zone in which the construction of East Asia and the stabilization of national defense are to be aimed at. After their completion there shall be a gradual expansion toward the construction of the Greater Co-Prosperity Sphere.

Outline of East Asiatic Administration. It is intended that the unification of Japan, Manchoukuo, and China in neighborly friendship be realized by the settlement of the Sino-Japanese problems through the crushing of hostile influences in the Chi-

From Ryusaku Tsunoda, Wm. Theodore de Bary, and Donald Keene, compilers, *Sources of the Japanese Tradition,* pp. 801-3 (New York: Columbia University Press).

nese interior, and through the construction of a new China in tune with the rapid construction of the Inner Sphere. Aggressive American and British influences in East Asia shall be driven out of the area of Indo-China and the South Seas, and this area shall be brought into our defense sphere. The war with Britain and America shall be prosecuted for that purpose.

The Russian aggressive influence in East Asia will be driven out. Eastern Siberia shall be cut off from the Soviet regime and included in our defense sphere. For this purpose, a war with the Soviets is expected. It is considered possible that this Northern problem may break out before the general settlement of the present Sino-Japanese and the Southern problems if the situation renders this unavoidable. Next the independence of Australia, India, etc. shall gradually be brought about. For this purpose, a recurrence of war with Britain and her allies is expected. The construction of a Greater Mongolian State is expected during the above phase. The construction of the Smaller Co-Prosperity Sphere is ex-pected to require at least twenty years from the present time.

The Building of the National Strength. Since the Japanese empire is the center and pioneer of Oriental moral and cultural reconstruction, the officials and people of this country must return to the spirit of the Orient and acquire a thorough understanding of the spirit of the national moral character.

In the economic construction of the country, Japanese and Manchurian national power shall first be consolidated, then the unification of Japan, Manchoukuo and China, shall be effected. . . . Thus a central industry will be constructed in East Asia, and the necessary relations established with the Southern Seas.

The standard for the construction of the national power and its military force, so as to meet the various situations that might affect the stages of East Asiatic administration and the national defense sphere, shall be so set as to be capable of driving off any British, American, Soviet or Chinese counter-influences in the future. . . .

SUGGESTIONS FOR ADDITIONAL READING

The 1931–45 period can be understood only in the general context of modern Japanese history. Hugh Borton's *Japan's Modern Century* (New York, 1955) is a good introduction. A more detailed study of modern Japanese politics is Chitoshi Yanaga's *Japan Since Perry* (New York, 1949); Robert Scalapino's *Democracy and the Party Movement in Pre-War Japan* (California, 1953) is a monograph focused on the reasons for the breakdown of democratic institutions and ideals in pre-war Japan. For the economic background the best general study is G. C. Allen's *A Short Economic History of Modern Japan* (London, 1946).

Nationalism in Japan by Delmer Brown (California, 1955) is a general treatment of the subject from the origins, but very useful for the period of the 1930s. In addition to the books from which the selections in this volume have been taken, the following can be recommended for their coverage of the 1931–45 period:

Richard Storry: *The Double Patriots* (London, 1957), a study of the ultra-nationalists in Japan and of their growing influence in the late 1920's and the 1930's.

Y. C. Maxon: *Control of Japanese Foreign Policy* (California, 1957), which concentrates on the civilian-military rivalry between 1930 and 1945.

Hugh Byas: *Government by Assassination* (New York, 1942), a foreign correspondent's lively description of the political developments in Japan that led to the Pacific War.

F. C. Jones: *Japan's New Order in East Asia* (London, 1954), which gives a detailed account of the rise and fall of the Japanese empire from 1937 to 1945.

Robert Butow: *Tojo and the Coming of the War* (Princeton, 1961), in which we learn about the period through a study of the Prime Minister who led his country into war against the West.

Readers who are interested in the development of nationalism and militarism after Japan's defeat may wish to consult *Nationalism and the Right Wing in Japan* (London, 1960), a study of post-war trends by Ivan Morris.